THE BUSINESS OF
PERSONAL FINANCE

This book is no ordinary personal finance book. It presents, in a highly accessible way, how to effectively understand and manage personal finances, avoiding debt and building for the future, and using straightforward tools and techniques developed in conjunction with business economics.

Fun to read, the book leverages core corporate finance principles in a way that helps people become more financially literate in their personal lives. The premise of this book—that personal and corporate finance can and should be learned together to improve financial wellness and know-how—is considered a breakthrough. Using approaches that have been tried, tested, and proven to work with individuals and employees, the authors apply common business activities like "due diligence," and tools, such as "financial statement analysis," to personal finance. This connection has not been presented before, either theoretically or practically. And yet it has the power to both transform how individuals successfully manage their own finances, and, at the same time, informs and educates them in the important aspects of the financial direction of the organizations in which they work.

This is a must-have book for those who are looking for a credible reference tool for how to effectively manage their own finances and for organizations seeking to assist their employees in good financial management, at every level, both in work and at home.

Joseph Calandro, Jr. is Managing Director of a global consulting firm, Fellow of the Gabelli Center for Global Security Analysis at Fordham University, and a contributing editor of *Strategy & Leadership*.

John Hoffmire is Research Associate, Kellogg College, University of Oxford, and an associate member of the Senior Common Room, Regent's Park College. He is also Chairman of Oxford Pharmaceuticals; Chairman of Cadence Innova; Founder of the Center on Business and Poverty; and Director and Chairman, Personal Finance Employee Education Fund.

"This short guide to personal finance is chock-full of experience-based economic wisdom. I wish I could have read it sixty years ago at the start of my career. Regardless of your age, read it now. Absorb its lessons. They will show you how to make better financial and life-cycle decisions to achieve personal financial wellness."

—Richard Sylla, co-author of
A History of Interest Rates, 4th Ed.,
Professor Emeritus of Economics, New York University;
Chairman of the Museum of American Finance (2010–2020)

"Joe Calandro and John Hoffmire have very effectively written about financial literacy in a way that is practical, accessible and academically strong. This is an excellent resource for those who wish to obtain a better grasp of, and improve, their personal finance."

—Susana Frazao Pinheiro, Head,
Healthcare and Life Sciences, School of Management,
University College London

"Financial independence is the cornerstone of personal freedom and this book provides the most succinct guide I've seen for wealth creation. I'm giving copies to all my children and grandchildren—those here and those to come!"

—John J. Sviokla, author of *The Self-Made Billionaire Effect:
How Extreme Producers Create Massive Value*,
PwC Principal (retired), and former
Associate Professor of Harvard Business School

"I really love the book. It is fresh. And the stories about the financial foibles of well-known celebrities are fascinating."

—Tom Garman,
Distinguished Professor Emeritus, Virginia Tech

THE BUSINESS OF PERSONAL FINANCE

HOW TO IMPROVE FINANCIAL WELLNESS

Joseph Calandro, Jr. and John Hoffmire

Routledge
Taylor & Francis Group

LONDON AND NEW YORK

Cover image: © Getty Images

First published 2022
by Routledge
4 Park Square, Milton Park, Abingdon, Oxon OX14 4RN

and by Routledge
605 Third Avenue, New York, NY 10158

Routledge is an imprint of the Taylor & Francis Group, an informa business

British Library Cataloguing-in-Publication Data
A catalogue record for this book is available from the British Library

Library of Congress Cataloging-in-Publication Data
Names: Calandro, Joseph, author. | Hoffmire, John, author.
Title: The business of personal finance : how to improve financial wellness / Joseph Calandro Jr., and John Hoffmire.
Description: 1 Editon. | New York, NY : Routledge, 2022. | Includes bibliographical references and index.
Identifiers: LCCN 2021055672 (print) | LCCN 2021055673 (ebook) | ISBN 9781032104560 (hardback) | ISBN 9781032104577 (paperback) | ISBN 9781003215417 (ebook)
Subjects: LCSH: Finance, Personal.
Classification: LCC HG179 .C295 2022 (print) | LCC HG179 (ebook) | DDC 332.024—dc23/eng/20220105
LC record available at https://lccn.loc.gov/2021055672
LC ebook record available at https://lccn.loc.gov/2021055673

ISBN: 978-1-032-10456-0 (hbk)
ISBN: 978-1-032-10457-7 (pbk)
ISBN: 978-1-003-21541-7 (ebk)

DOI: 10.4324/9781003215417

Typeset in Bembo
by Apex CoVantage, LLC

From Joe: For Terilyn, for the hat trick. And for Alyse, who inspired it all.

From John: With much thanks to Shelley, Kate, James, and Peter. You mean the world to me.

CONTENTS

ACKNOWLEDGMENTS

While the act of writing is an individual one, a great many people have helped us along the way. Our personal finance writing started with newspaper columns, which were published by the *Telegraph Herald*. We would like to thank the *Telegraph Herald* for supporting our writing, and for their permission to develop and rewrite the material from their columns in this manuscript.

We would like to thank the following people for reviewing and endorsing our manuscript: Tom Garman, Jim Goodman, James Russell Kelly, Juneen Belknap Kirk, Susana Frazao Pinheiro, Sara Roth, Joe Saari, Ken Serwinski, John J. Sviokla, and Richard Sylla.

We would also like to acknowledge: Alistair Aitchison, Gary Ashby, Jim Bado, Jane Barrett, Helaman Barrios, Brad Barron, Ted Beck, Ian Bird, Don Blandin, Michael Brown, Joanna Butler, Sris Chatterjee, Judith Cohart, Michael Collins, Scott Cook, Liz Davidson, Dan and Ellen De Magistris, Vincent DiRaddo, Scott Drake, Ceilidh Erikson, Alex Eu, Scott Evoy, Greg Galeaz, Tom Garman, Francis Goss, Mike Gutter, Scott Hammond, Shelley Hammond, Tom Harms, Stephanie Harrill, George Hofheimer, Bill Horan, Cathy Ivancic, Len Janeski, Jaimes Johnson, James Russell Kelly, Paul Kundert, Ted Lakkides, Darren Laverty, Dave Mancl, Chris Manning, Mike Marco, Scott McMillen, John Menke, Mark Meyer, Matthew Mitten, Alex Moss, Christine Myers, Tim O'Neil, Peter Pescatore, Simon Pickerill, Carmen Porco, Joe Porto, Nick Pritchard, Mark and Deb Purowitz, Brenda Purschke, Pat Quirk, Francois Ramette, Loren Rodgers, Corey Rosen, Joe Saari, Ken Serwinski, Zia Shannon, Karl Scholz, Sarah Shirley, Kevin Shiiba, Jim Steiker, Kristen Stringer, Tim Sumiek, Jennifer Tescher, John

Thompson, Peter Tufano, Adam Turville, Ken Wanko, Craig Williams, Craig Wilson, and Jamie Yoder.

Joe would also like to thank his family for their continued support of his research and his writing, particularly his wife and daughter, Terilyn and Alyse, in-laws Larry and Dolores Vecchione, aunt Carol Bickley, and uncle and aunt Jim and Linda Wilson.

John would like to express his appreciation to his family. Shelley, Kate, and James have watched and participated in financial wellness experiments for more than 25 years. Peter, Kate's husband, is a great poverty alleviation researcher in his own right.

INTRODUCTION

We wrote this book for two primary reasons. First, we would like to help people who desire to responsibly improve their financial position. Second, we would like to assist those who are trying to help others to develop better personal financial wellness skills.

As we write these words, various stock markets around the world are somewhat uncertain, but even before that, on a basic level, we knew that many people were struggling financially. Many have too much debt. Some suffer from health issues caused by stressful financial concerns. And for others, the stressful concerns have negatively impacted their work performance and their personal relationships, including and especially family relationships.

We have an added concern here: the world of business and finance does not seem stable. So much is changing from historical norms: a deep global recession, which led to multi-trillion-dollar governmental budget deficits, continuous monetary stimulus, historically low interest rates, and ever greater levels of income inequality. Furthermore, during the aftermath of the 2007–2008 Great Recession, we do not feel that, in general, governments, corporations, or individuals learned enough, or made the necessary changes to prevent distress in the event of a future financial crisis—and there is *always* a next financial crisis. As we write this, the financial markets seem to have recovered from the volatility of March 2020 that was generated from the Covid-19 pandemic, but it is far from clear that another bout of volatility is not around the corner.

We hope that this book helps its readers to strengthen their financial health during the current stressful financial environment, as well as into the future. In the chapters that follow, we will expand on

DOI: 10.4324/9781003215417-1

select topics to inform a wide variety of people how they can practically enhance their financial position, in both good macroeconomics times and difficult ones.

Two things differentiate our book from many other personal finance books that have been published. The first is that our discussion frequently involves practical technical considerations. For example, we think it is important that people truly understand financial concepts such as "interest rates" and "compound interest," and that they know how to track and use them over time. With a little effort, everyone can do this.

Second, we apply common business activities like "due diligence" and tools, such as financial statement analysis, to personal finance. Incredibly, this connection has not yet been rigorously made before, either theoretically or practically, as far as we are aware. The consequences of this have been significant in a number of cases. For example, we know several chief financial officers (CFOs) and chief investment officers (CIOs) who did things from a personal finance perspective that they would never do professionally, which caused them significant levels of personal distress. This is unfortunate because "good finance" applies equally to both businesses and people, as we will show in the chapters that follow this introduction.

In Chapter 1 we kick things off by offering our "Ten Commandments" of financial wellness, along with profiles of well-known historical figures—such as Winston Churchill and Mark Twain—who acted in ways contrary to the commandments and suffered financially as a result. We have found that profiles like these are important from an educational perspective because many people seem more willing to acknowledge that they have a personal finance issue if they know there are other people, including and especially celebrities, who suffer from the same kinds of issues.

In Chapter 2 we address the topics of spending, saving, and interest. We show how to practically evaluate the "value" claimed by many pitchmen, and how to avoid impulse purchases, which can lead to excessive spending. We then discuss saving, and practically explain interest rates and the power of the popular "Rule of 72" to appreciate the key concept of "compound interest." A takeaway of this chapter is the importance of tracking the interest rates that one pays, and then comparing them to the interest rates that one earns. Needless to say, it is beneficial to limit the former while compounding the latter.

Many people save money, and strive to create wealth, through their jobs. Obviously, not all jobs are created equally, which is a challenge that all employees must wrestle with. To help address this challenge, Chapter 3 discusses the importance of employee stock ownership plans (ESOPs) as well as the managerial technique open book management (OPM). Businesses that offer ESOPs and that are run according to OBM could prove highly attractive to prospective employees.

Chapter 4 pertains to strategy and prices. While many people know that strategy is a key business function, few look at personal finance strategically. This chapter practically explains how to do so. It then profiles the different kinds of prices—premium, retail, and discount prices—and how people can be more price conscious as both buyers and sellers.

Chapter 5 profiles the important subject of risk management. Specifically, it shows how to practically mitigate the risk of losing a job, and various ways to manage personal investment risk. One way to manage personal investment risk is to avoid fraudulent investors. To facilitate this, we profile several risk-management lessons that emerged out of the infamous Bernie Madoff Ponzi scheme, which all can be widely and practically employed.

Chapter 6 continues the discussion on risk management, but with respect to cyber risk, which is important because our society is becoming increasingly digital. While digitization brings many benefits, it also generates a number of cyber-related risks. This chapter profiles ways that cyber risk can be practically managed.

Chapter 7 is, in many ways, the heart and soul of the book. It is also one of the key differences between this book and many other personal finance books. This chapter profiles the three financial statements of corporate finance—the income statement, cash flow statement, and balance sheet—and shows how the statements can be practically applied to personal finance. While simple in its construction, this linkage is incredibly powerful, and has not been made before. The concepts introduced in this chapter will be used in future chapters.

Chapter 8 profiles small business finance. Nearly half of all small business failures occur due to financial issues. Following the last chapter, this chapter profiles several ways that the three financial statements can be used by small business owners to manage their finances more efficiently. While financial statement expertise alone will not ensure a successful small business, it will go a very long way in helping to ensure that a successful small business remains successful over time.

Chapter 9 pertains to your home. For many people, buying a house is the largest purchase that they will ever make. As a result, most home purchases are financed through a mortgage, which is typically payable over 20 to 30 years. This chapter profiles the personal finance implications of owning a home outright, and how "mortgage burning parties" are a good practice to bring back. Some people who have paid off their homes have turned to a "reverse mortgage" to help cover financial shortfalls that they are experiencing. We profile some of the things people should consider if they are evaluating a reverse mortgage.

Chapter 10 covers the subject of consumer credit or debt. If you are going to use credit, you should use it sparingly, and be well-informed of the terms of that use, including initial interest rates as well as rate reset provisions. The only way to accomplish this is to read the fine print of the credit documents that you have been provided. This sounds easy to do, and it is relatively easy to do, but many people simply do not do it.

Chapter 11 profiles the connection between physical wellness and financial wellness. While getting, and staying, in shape physically is generally very popular these days, the connection between physical and financial wellness is frequently ignored. This is a mistake because being in "financial shape" can greatly reduce stress levels. It is well known that stress can lead to a variety of severe illnesses. This chapter profiles two practical measures of financial wellness. It also discusses ways to maintain wellness by having career back-up plans, and in situations where disabled dependents must be cared for.

Chapter 12 turns to the all-important subject of personal investing. Diversification is essential to responsible long-term personal investing, and as a result, this chapter offers several practical suggestions that can be considered when a personal diversification strategy is being formulated. The chapter also addresses how financial guarantees can be evaluated, which is important as many investment scams make the claim of some form of "guarantee." Understanding how to differentiate a valid from an invalid financial guarantee is an important part of a long-term personal investing strategy.

Chapter 13 turns to other kinds of personal investments such as how to evaluate the merits of a university education, and how to think about charitable donations.

In the Conclusion, we offer five more commandments of financial wellness to go-along with our original ten commandments from Chapter 1. We then conclude the book with a brief case study of a person who illustrates many of the concepts that are profiled in the book.

We note that some level of repetition is inevitable in personal finance books, and in this book such repetition is very much intentional. We hope that it does not distract from our message, and that it proves useful.

1

THE "TEN COMMANDMENTS" OF FINANCIAL WELLNESS

We were recently speaking with someone about the personal financial challenges that we have observed over the years from a wide variety of people. Toward the end of our conversation, the person we were speaking with stated that, "You know, it would be very helpful if you could distill key personal finance 'rules' into a grand list that is easy to follow. Sort of like a set of personal finance 'commandments.'"

We thought this was a great idea.

Thinking through all of the various personal finance "rules" that we know of resulted in the following list of "Ten Commandments" of financial wellness, which we offer in no particular order (unlike the original Ten Commandments):

1. The house you live in is your home, it is NOT a source of equity to "unlock" or an ATM-like repository of cash to spend. Your home is where you and your family live. Therefore, you should not use it as collateral for any loan outside of a first mortgage, absent some dire circumstance. To repeat, absent something dire, you should *never* put your home financially at risk.

2. Whenever you make a purchase, even a large purchase like a home or car, try to pay discount prices whenever possible. It will likely take time to find favorably priced assets and goods, but it is well worth both your time and your effort to do so. Sometimes a great "deal" will fall into your lap, but that is the exception rather than the rule. Normally, you have to work at it to find a discount.

3. Pay close attention to interest rates. This applies to both the interest rates that you pay (such as mortgage rates, car loan rates,

DOI: 10.4324/9781003215417-2

and credit card rates) and the interest rates that you earn (from bank savings accounts, 401k plans, and individual retirement accounts). You should strive to earn more in interest income than you pay out in interest expense over time. The only way to accomplish this is to continuously work at it.

4 <u>Limit the purchase of luxury goods and fund such purchases with cash rather than credit to the extent that you can</u>. In general, you should only use consumer credit sparingly, and remember to watch the credit terms as well as the interest rates that you are charged when you do use it (as noted in commandment 3).

5 <u>Saving money is important</u>. The act of saving gets the power of "compounding" (or interest paid on interest, and investment returns that are earned on prior investment returns) working for you over time. Therefore, the sooner that you start to save, the better—even if the amounts that you save are small.

6 <u>Don't ever forget that there is NO easy way to become wealthy</u>. This is particularly important to remember when you are dealing with someone who tells you that they have a simple or easy way for you to become wealthy. People who say things like this either do not know what they are talking about and/or they are fraudsters. Whatever else you do after reading this book, please do *not* ignore this commandment!

7 <u>Size matters</u>. So, absent some very compelling reason, you should generally only invest with large money management firms. Large firms tend to have large assets of their own, and they have large amounts of insurance coverage to protect those assets if they are sued. Having assets and insurance available to pay legal judgments will help to mitigate the risk of fraud or loss if something goes wrong. Regrettably, things can, and often do, go wrong with investments for any number of reasons.

8 <u>Do not put all your investment eggs into one basket</u>. To the extent that your savings portfolio begins to grow, you should generally diversify your investment funds across different money management firms and asset classes. For example, have one money management firm invest stocks for you and another money management firm invest bonds for you. You should generally never have just one firm managing all your money.

9 <u>Ignore "the Joneses."</u> Many people feel under pressure to keep up with the spending patterns of family, friends, and celebrities.

This is a mistake for a variety of reasons, primary amongst these is that the people you may be trying to keep up with may not have made well-thought-out purchases and/or may not have funded their purchases well. Therefore, you should fund the lifestyle that YOU want, not the one that you think someone else has.

10 If you come to be defrauded, contact law enforcement officials immediately. Do not delay because of feelings of embarrassment. You should never feel embarrassed, but rather take action quickly in the hope that you will get at least some of your money back, and that you will help to bring the fraudster to justice as quickly as possible.

These commandments are obviously not dogmatic commandments like the original Ten Commandments. Rather, they are a set of practical guidelines that we have found useful precisely because we have seen what can happen when they are not followed. Unfortunately, many of these commandments are frequently not followed; in fact, some people seem hardwired to act in directly opposite ways. For example, many people continue to use their homes as collateral to fund luxury goods, which they often buy at high-to-premium prices (in contrast to commandments 1, 2, and 4).

Similarly, many people do not track the interest rates that they pay, and many more do not keep track of the difference between the rates that they pay and the rates that they earn over time. This is contrary to commandment 3, which often prevents these people from putting the power of compounding to work (commandment 5).

We have found that once someone consistently breaks one or more of these commandments, a bad habit can form leading to personal financial issues over time. Significantly, everyone is at risk of having such issues, including the rich and famous, a few of whom who we will profile in the following sections.

PERSONAL FINANCIAL ISSUES OF THE "RICH AND FAMOUS"

As noted earlier, bad habits are at the center of many financial issues. We define a *financial bad habit* as having two attributes: The first is recurrent violations of one or more of our Ten Commandments of financial wellness. The second attribute is that a violation causes a financial problem in someone's life: personal, professional, or both. Significantly, a bad habit can worsen over time. For example, a person who consistently buys luxury goods may come to need the "rush" of shopping.

Another example is a person who, as a one-shot deal, mortgages their home to invest in a "sure thing" investment, which turns out to be a fraud. Anyone who has watched the popular television show, *American Greed*, has seen many examples of scenarios like this. Sadly, we know several people who thought they were investing in a "sure thing" who lost all of their money.

It is important to understand that everyone is at risk of developing a financial bad habit if care is not taken to prevent it. In fact, some of the most successful people across history have developed such habits. This is important from an educational perspective because we have found that many people are willing to acknowledge that they have a personal finance issue if they know there are others, especially celebrities, who suffer from the same kinds of problems.

What follows are two detailed vignettes about famous people who had significant personal finance issues. In each case, we identify the financial issues that are related to our "commandments," which led to financial difficulties. We begin with one of the most magnetic and popular personalities of the 20th century, Winston Churchill.

WINSTON CHURCHILL

Many political and military books have been written about Winston Churchill being a strategically effective leader. Therefore, we were both pleasantly surprised when we read a recently published book that chronicled Mr. Churchill's life from a personal finance perspective, and in so doing profiled many of his financial warts.

David Lough's superb book, *No More Champagne: Churchill & His Money* (New York: Picador, 2015), gets its title from something that Mr. Churchill once said regarding the need to cut back on his and his family's excessive spending, especially alcohol-related spending. For example, Mr. Lough reported that Churchill spent approximately $158,688 per year (£104,400 at the time of Lough's writing) on wine.

There is a great deal that can be learned from Mr. Lough's book. Here are some of our observations that pertain to personal finance in general.

We live in an age of consumerism that strongly encourages spending instead of thrift. The life of Winston Churchill was in many ways a life of spending, and not just spending on wine. Churchill enjoyed gambling, trading risky stocks, and overspending on home improvements. Indeed, his luxury-based spending was so excessive that he had to go, and remain, deeply into debt to fund it throughout his life.

To try to control his spending, Churchill prepared numerous personal budgets. However, he frequently overestimated his sources of income and he underestimated his costs. He also did not exercise the discipline needed to successfully follow his budgets. Needless to say, budgets only work when they are as accurate as possible and when they are followed.

Churchill's excessive spending habits and heavy debt-loads eventually generated financial distress. In fact, his financial position was so precarious on two separate occasions that he had to be privately bailed out to prevent bankruptcy. Celebrity and political success are simply no substitute for frugality and being fiscally conservative.

Churchill also occasionally sought "gifts" to mitigate his financial situation. Frankly, such behavior is not ethical. However, people under financial distress sometimes do things that they would not otherwise do. For example, we know of several people who "padded" their corporate expense accounts over a number of years to pick up a little extra money from their employers. While such padding may seem innocent to some people, it is stealing. One of these person's thefts eventually caught up to him and he was fired. If you find yourself under financial pressure, you should sacrifice your spending not your ethics.

Like many people, Winston Churchill gambled. To the extent that gambling is approached as entertainment and budgeted for, it could have a place in a personal budget, although we generally discourage it. Many people delude themselves into believing that gambling is a source of income, instead of a cost. The science of statistics is very clear that only "the house" profits from gambling over time.[1]

Churchill also traded stocks based on "tips" that he received from a variety of people, including preeminent traders of his day such as the legendary Bernard Baruch.[2] However, no one can trade successfully over time on tips: Churchill could not, we cannot, and neither can you.

One area of personal finance where Mr. Churchill clearly excelled was tax management. He worked incredibly hard to minimize his tax liability over time, which may sound surprising to some people given how long Churchill worked in government. Be that as it may, this is a very good practice that we should all follow. However, many people are not knowledgeable of even the most basic aspects of tax management, such as the mechanics of filing a tax return, and they do not have a basic understanding of tax terms and definitions. There are practical courses available from tax service providers on these subjects, and they are well worth your time.

We live in an era of ever-increasing amounts of government intervention and activity, so we should all have at least a basic understanding of how our governments—local, state, and federal—fund their activities, and how that funding impacts us via the tax code.

In closing this profile, the aspect of Churchill's example that strikes us most is the difference between how strategically effective he was in politics, foreign affairs, and managing the United Kingdom's military during World War II versus how strategically disastrous he was from a personal finance perspective. Skill in one area, even to the point of mastery, simply does not equate to skill in another area, and that includes personal finance.

MARK TWAIN

Like many people, we are Mark Twain fans. For one of us, though, this interest led to a recent trip to Hartford, Connecticut, and a visit to Twain's historic home.

Browsing through the gift shop after the tour, the following book caught our attention, *Ignorance, Confidence, and Filthy Rich Friends: The Business Adventures of Mark Twain, Chronic Speculator and Entrepreneur* (Hoboken, New Jersey: Wiley, 2007) by Peter Krass. This book also contains many useful personal finance insights.

Samuel Clemens, which is Mark Twain's real name, was raised in poverty. One of the reasons why his family was poor was that his father went heavily into debt to speculate on land. His speculations, like so very many other speculations before and after his, were not successful and his family suffered financially as a result. This experience fostered in young Sam Clemens a deep aversion to debt.

Nevertheless, Clemens went into debt when he got older to pursue certain commercial interests, which resulted in bankruptcy and years of hard work to settle his debts. The perils of excessive debt involve lessons that, unfortunately, need to be continuously learned (and, in some cases, re-learned) by many people over time.

Fortunately, Clemens developed a strong work ethic when he was young. He did not like being poor, and he was determined to work hard to both create and sustain wealth so that he would no longer be poor. This he accomplished, and by so doing he set an example that we should all seek to emulate.

However, like his father before him, Clemens was a speculative dreamer. While dreaming can help to inspire great novels, it generally does not result in successful investing, especially over time.

For example, many speculations that Clemens ventured into were outright frauds. To make matters worse, Clemens exacerbated his losses by doing exactly what so many others have done and continue to do: Throw good money after bad in the hope that doing so will help to "turn things around." However, it *never* makes economic sense to continue to fund a fraud in the hopes of reversing one's fortunes.

In both Clemens's time, and in our time, if someone is defrauded, they should immediately contact the authorities, possibly with the assistance of legal counsel. While the law was far less complex in Clemens's time, he nevertheless made extensive use of counsel to protect his legal rights, which is a practice that should be broadly followed.

Clemens finally came to see the folly of speculation and famously observed that, "There are two times in a man's life when he should not speculate: when he can't afford it, and when he can." We agree!

Despite his incredible success as an author and entertainer, Clemens tended to view himself more as a businessman. Some of his business ventures experienced success in generating significant revenue. For example, he started a firm that published, in two volumes, the *Personal Memoirs of U.S. Grant* (New York: Charles L. Webster & Company, 1885). This book was an international best-seller, and it has become a classic that is widely read to this day (for example, it is one of our favorite books). Furthermore, the marketing strategy that Clemens implemented to promote Grant's book was highly innovative, and it continues to be studied.[3]

However, despite all this success, Clemens did not profit from publishing Grant's memoirs. One of the reasons why pertains to the royalties agreement that he offered to General Grant. While other publishers offered Grant a 10 percent royalty, Clemens offered Grant an astounding 70 percent royalty. Clearly, he was not price conscious and suffered professionally as a result.

In his later years, Clemens met and befriended a highly successful Standard Oil executive by the name of Henry "Hell Hound" Rogers. As his nickname betrays, Rogers was a no-nonsense executive who successfully advised Clemens on many business and financial issues. While few of us have personal friends of such stature and capability, we can all make use of experts (such as licensed professional advisors) to help inform our financial decision-making.

SPORTS, MEDIA PERSONALITIES, LOTTERY WINNERS, AND EVEN EXECUTIVES!

Politicians and authors are obviously not the only celebrities to suffer financially. Professional athletes have also had financial issues across time. Consider Jack Dempsey, who became the heavyweight boxing champion in the year 1919, on the eve of the infamous "roaring twenties." Dempsey made a great deal of money from professional boxing. Evidence of this is that he fought in the first $1 million and $2 million matches in boxing history, as measured by the size of the gate revenues. However, he lived a lavish lifestyle and he also speculated on margin, or debt, based on the erroneous investment advice that he was getting at the time. As a result, Dempsey was wiped out financially during the infamous stock market crash of 1929, and the subsequent "Great Depression."

To recover, Dempsey returned to the boxing ring where, according to his autobiography, he "boxed forty-two opponents over a period of thirty days." Such a strategy would, most certainly, not be allowed today for health reasons. He also served as a boxing referee and basically did whatever he could to earn money. Such activities eventually led to the opening of the popular *Jack Dempsey's Restaurant*, and the restoration of his financial position.

Boxing aficionados frequently consider Dempsey one of the greatest boxers of all time. Another boxer mentioned in such discussions is, of course, Muhammad Ali.

One thing that non-boxers frequently fail to appreciate is the business-side of professional boxing. For example, how do you get many people to pay good money to see two adults beat each other up? It is not as easy as you may think, but Ali was an absolute master at it. So much so that he earned a great deal of money over his long and illustrious boxing career.

However, lavish spending and speculative business ventures (such as "Champ Burger" fast food restaurants, "Mr. Champ's" soda, several failed movies deals, and other business failures) severely eroded his financial resources. After this occurred, Ali made several very astute business moves, including the sale of his name and image, which dramatically improved his financial position. Obviously, such moves are not an option for ordinary people like us. Therefore, we must take care of ourselves financially the old fashioned way—by doing the things that make sense from a conservative personal finance perspective consistently over time.

Thus far we have profiled only historical celebrities, but that does not mean more modern celebrities have not had personal finance issues. Consider the article, "13 celebrities who have struggled with money," which was published on December 6, 2018 by *Insider* (www.insider.com/celebrities-lost-money-bankruptcy-debt-2018-7). The celebrities profiled in this article include some of most popular today: Johnny Depp, Toni Braxton, Da Bratt, Mike Tyson, Cyndi Lauper, Willie Nelson, Debbie Reynolds, 50 Cent, Larry King, Kim Basinger, Marvin Gaye, Teresa and Joe Giudice, and Drake Bell.

Even abnormally lucky people can fall prey to financial issues. Consider information that has been uncovered in a study conducted by *Wolf Street*, which found that nearly a third of big lottery winners go on to declare bankruptcy. This study covers a waterfront of mistakes and illustrates breaches of all ten of our "commandments" of financial wellness.[4]

When we speak with people about the financial travails of some lottery winners, we sometimes get the reply, "Well, what do you expect? So-and-so isn't educated; never went to college, let alone business school." Such comments may be factually accurate but, as noted earlier, we know many examples of former chief executive officers (CEOs), chief operating officers (COOs), chief financial officers (CFOs), and even chief investment officers (CIOs) who have suffered from personal financial issues due to breaching one or more of our commandments of financial wellness.

In closing, as we have noted, financial issues can, and often do, affect virtually anyone. Furthermore, professional success—even professional business success—does not always lead to long-term financial wellness. In contrast, we have found that successful personal finance habits are learned and fostered, frequently over a lifetime. We created our "Ten Commandments" of financial wellness to help facilitate this learning.

NOTES

1 There are exceptions to this statement such as, for example, card count-ing in the game of blackjack, as first described by Ed Thorp in his seminal book, *Beat the Dealer* (New York: Vintage, 1966 [1962]). Such strategies work because they change the odds of gambling, which is why casinos put so much effort into preventing people who are skilled at such strategies from gambling on their property. The mathematical skill required to gamble like this is extremely high, and it is also fraught with various risks, which make it generally unsustainable over time.

2 For more information on Baruch see James Grant, *Bernard Baruch: The Adven-tures of a Wall Street Legend* (New York: Wiley, 1997).

3 For a short and highly readable example see Bill Murphy, Jr., "Mark Twain Was a Marketing Genius: America's Greatest Author Had Some Brilliant Ideas," *Inc.*, November 5 (2013), www.inc.com/bill-murphy-jr/mark-twain-was-a-marketing-genius.html

4 Safehaven, "Nearly One-Third of U.S. Lottery Winners Declare Bank-ruptcy," *Wolf Street*, April 17 (2018), https://wolfstreet.com/2018/04/17/nearly-one-third-of-u-s-lottery-winners-declare-bankruptcy/

2

SPENDING, SAVING, AND INTEREST

We recently spoke with several economists about our personal finance research and writings. One of them recommended that we consider writing about people continuously buying things that they do not need. He is so passionate about this topic that he has a framed picture of someone, positioned prominently on his desk, who was lured into buying a great many things that they did not need over the years. The picture is a constant reminder to not buy un-needed stuff.

One of the reasons why people seem to habitually purchase unneeded items is that they are led to believe that they are getting a "deal." However, just because something is marketed as a deal does not mean that it is one.

For example, television commercial pitchmen often say things like, "And if you call within the next 10 minutes, we will throw in another product absolutely free. This is a $40 value, but you have to call now!"

The intention of pitches like this is to entice *impulse buying*, which is an unplanned, spur-of-the-moment purchase. The impulse "nudge" in this commercial is the offer of a $40 value within a fixed amount of time. But what exactly is "a $40 value?"

From an economic perspective, if something is a $40 value it generally means that you can relatively quickly turn the "value" into $40 cash. However, this is likely not what pitchmen, and other aggressive sales people, mean when they use this language.

Pitchmen are in the business of convincing individuals to buy their products. Notice that we did not say that they are in the business of marketing their products to the people who may really need them. Pitchmen generally want as many people to buy their products as

DOI: 10.4324/9781003215417-3

possible, and they frame their sales pitches to have this affect. Now, with this mind, let's revisit the "$40 value pitch."

At least two aspects of pitches like this are important. First is a fixed-offer timeframe, such as the 10-minute timeframe mentioned in our example, which rarely, if ever, holds firm; in other words, you can likely call later and get the exact same deal. In fact, we have done this on several occasions and were offered the same deal, "but only if you buy right now!"

Second, ask yourself what makes a deal special? Generally, a deal is special if it is available to a few people. Why, then, would someone pay you $40 cash when anyone could call the same number you did and get the exact same deal? Questions like this suggest people may not understand what is meant by the term "value."

Pitchmen, and the bosses who employ them, understand there is often confusion around the term value, and this allows them to exaggerate the "value" of the products they pitch. In fact, many of them often lie about their product's value. This, sadly, is a fact of life that we all must continuously deal with in finance—both corporate and personal.

We do not suggest you call pitchmen liars, but we do want you to be cynical about *all* claims of value. To develop a greater level of cynicism about pitches, let us delve into the concept of value.

A dictionary defines *value* as, "The worth of something to its owner." This is obviously not a very insightful definition, but it does underscore the important fact that value—the value of everything, in fact—is inherently subjective. This means that value can be defined in various ways. Consequently, people can—and oftentimes do—define value differently, sometimes extremely differently. One practical implication of this is that pitchmen tend to define value far more broadly than more financially conservative and responsible people do.

Consequently, for our purposes here, we suggest that you develop a hard-nosed definition of value as the price you have to pay for something that you really need at the time you really need it. We want you to consider that salespeople who may be trying to convince you to use a more aggressive definition might, at the very least, be exaggerating.

Some context before we move on: It is natural to want a "deal" when you are buying things. Salespeople know this and construct their pitches accordingly. They profile their products, services, and prices in the most favorable and broadest light possible. In fact, this is what they are paid to do. With this in mind, here are some things to consider when evaluating sales pitches in general.

First, you should avoid making impulse purchases. To do this, simply wait 24 hours (or longer) before you buy something that attracts your attention. Over time this will help to prevent unwise purchases.

If, after waiting 24 hours or so, you decide that you would still like to make a purchase, you should validate all claims of value carefully. In other words, determine exactly how a salesperson is defining value, and then determine if that definition applies to you. In corporate finance, this process is called *due diligence*, which is a method of taking reasonable steps to validate key financial claims and assumptions when you are considering a purchase. Effective due diligence is a critical corporate and personal finance safeguard.

Next, you should determine how you are going to realize the value. In the previous example, the pitchman's "value proposition" is a two-for-the-price-of-one offer. Before accepting such an offer, you should determine what you are going to do with the second item: Are you going to use it, sell it, or give it to someone else? If you do not need or want the second item, perhaps the seller will negotiate on the price so that instead of getting two-for-the-price-of-one, you can buy one product for half price? We have tried this in the past and it has rarely worked, but when it has worked, the "deal" worked for us.

If, after following these suggestions, you doubt whether a sales pitch creates "value" for you, then it isn't a "deal" and as such you should not purchase anything. You can always buy the product later if a true deal emerges.

TIME PREFERENCE AND INTEREST RATES

Whether to buy something now or later is a key decision that we all face. It is natural to want nice things "today." However, as we just discussed, it is not always economically wise to buy something today.

People who use their money well tend to buy things that they truly need at discount or otherwise reasonable prices, and then they save the rest of their money so that they will be able to buy things economically in the future. This practice is known as *thrift*, and it very much seems to be a dying art. What many people do not readily understand is that "time," and one's "time preference," is at the center of thrift.

If you are going to postpone buying something today, and instead save for the future, you generally have a longer time preference, and will be paid for your willingness to wait. In other words, you will earn money on your savings until you decide to spend it sometime in the future. The money that you earn while you are saving for the proverbial "rainy day" is a function of interest rates. No matter what you do in finance, from either a business or personal perspective, interest rates will be at the center of it. For example:

- If you choose to spend all your money in the present and therefore not save anything, which is an extremely immediate time preference, you should at least know the interest rates that you are giving up, to fund your spending.
- If you are buying things today on credit, which is also an immediate time preference, you will be charged an interest rate. Understanding what this rate is, and how much it will cost you over time, is very important.
- If you buy relatively little today and therefore save most of what you earn, which is a very long-term time preference, you will need to determine if the interest rate you are earning adequately compensates you for the "lost utility" of your delayed purchases.

Many people use credit to fund at least some of their purchases; however, relatively few people understand and carefully track the interest rate(s) that they pay for the credit that they use. This is a very big mistake. The interest that you pay to fund your purchases is a cost, and like all costs, it can grow uncomfortably large if it is not carefully and continuously managed.

If you both use credit and save money, you should track and compare the interest rates that you pay with the interest rates that you earn. Specifically, you should strive to lower the former and increase the latter to the extent that you can. This is not easy to do. For example, at the time of this writing, many credit cards have annual interest rates of over 20 percent while bank savings accounts have annual interest rates of less than 1 percent.

The reasons for this discrepancy, which involve the governmental regulations and policies of both political parties in the United States, are not a subject of this book. The nature of the discrepancy, however, is at the heart of this book. In short, strive to limit the amount of money that you pay in interest while striving to conservatively earn as much interest as you can. In other words, strive for positive *net interest*, which is the difference between the amount of interest that you earn less the amount of interest that you pay. Doing so will help to put the miracle of compounding to work for you, which is the subject that we turn to next.

COMPOUNDING

All investments play out over time. Therefore, the phenomena of interest and other returns "compounding over time" is extremely important. By "compounding" we mean interest that is paid on interest, and investment returns that are earned on prior investment returns. Another way to explain this is that compounding is like reinvesting and making money off your profits. If this seems a little confusing, please stay with us until it becomes clear. To understand why, consider that Albert Einstein himself thought compounding was the eighth wonder of the world. He noted that those who understand compound interest, earn it, while those who do not understand it, pay it.[1]

Thankfully, we do not have to be as smart as Albert Einstein to understand the miracle of compounding. One way to help visualize it is through the popular "Rule of 72." We often use this "rule" to explain compounding to family members and friends by way of the following example.

First, we ask how many years it will take $1 to double at an annual interest rate of 50 percent. Most people reasonably respond, "Two years." When we ask them to explain how they came up with their answer, they often reply: "50 percent interest in year one plus 50 percent interest in year two equals $1, which when added to the $1 that we started with equals $2. Double the investment."

We then reply: "Yes, but in the second year you are also earning interest on the interest that you earned in the first year, which your answer did not include. Therefore, the actual number of years it takes to double in this example is approximately 1.5 years." To understand why, you simply divide 72 by 50 (the interest rate in our example), which equals 1.44 or approximately 1.5 years.

There are obviously limitations with quick-and-dirty calculations like the "Rule of 72." A key benefit, though, is that such calculations can be very useful for personal investment planning. To understand how, first consider Table 2.1.

Information like that found in the table begs a rather obvious investing question: How can higher returns be earned over time so that money will double at a faster rate?

One way to address such questions is to compare current investment alternatives with the *total returns*, or interest rates plus price appreciation (or depreciation) being earned in the financial markets, which is easy to do. For example, Table 2.2 profiles seven widely

Table 2.1 Basic Compound Interest Calculations

Interest Rate:	1.5%	2.5%	3.5%	6.0%	10.0%
Years to Double:	48	29	21	12	7

Note: "Years to Double" in the bottom row were calculated using the "Rule of 72," and have been rounded.

Table 2.2 Select Fixed Income Indices

		YIELD (%), 52-WEEK RANGE		
	YTD total return (%)	Latest	Low	High
Broad Market Bloomberg Barclays Indices				
U.S. Government/Credit	4.71	1.58	1.58	3.16
U.S. Aggregate	3.92	1.66	1.66	3.22
U.S. Corporate Indexes Bloomberg Barclays Indices				
U.S. Corporate	3.77	2.4	2.4	3.92
Intermediate	2.54	1.93	1.93	3.55
Long-term	6.01	3.22	3.22	4.69
Double-A-rated (AA)	4.05	1.9	1.9	3.29
Triple-B-rated (Baa)	3.32	2.72	2.71	4.28

Source: *Wall Street Journal Markets*, www.wsj.com/market-data/bonds/benchmarks Accessed on March 3, 2020 so it is *not* current financial data, and as such is displayed for illustration only.

followed bond indices. As can be seen, these bond indices fall within the 2.5 percent to 6.0 percent total return range, which means that their "years to double," per Table 2.1, range from approximately 12 to 29 years. This is a long time, and as a result some people may be tempted to undertake riskier investments in the hopes of earning higher returns.

Many of the people who succumb to such temptations likely do not consider the "compounding risks" involved. To explain, if you lose money in a year (or in a number of years), it can take a very long time to earn that money back, even with the power of compounding. Therefore, the first rule of personal investing is to not lose money, which is like the first rule of medicine: "first, do no harm." Following this rule may not seem exciting, but it will help to ensure that you do not lose the money that you worked so hard to earn in the first place. This is especially true for older people, even more so when they are investing in financial markets that have reached historically high levels.

In closing this chapter, it is important to observe that the way most people save money for investment purposes, and strive to create wealth, is through their job. Therefore, that is the topic we will turn to in the next chapter.

NOTE

1 James Rabinovich, "Leverage the Power of Compounding Interest," *Investing Tips 360*, March 4 (2014), www.investingtips360.com/leverage-the-power-of-compounding-interest/

OWNERSHIP AND OPEN BOOK MANAGEMENT

It probably came through in the last chapter that it is very difficult to make a great deal of money in the financial markets. One potential way around this difficulty, if you are an employee, is to work for a company that offers some form of employee ownership. There are several types of employee stock ownership plans (ESOPs), but for our purposes, we will put them into two categories. First, ESOPs with a capital "E" usually refer to employee ownership represented in the form of a retirement plan subject to guidelines set forth by the Internal Revenue Service and the U.S. Department of Labor. Second, ESOPs with a small "e" consist of a wide variety of plans that include stock bonuses, stock options, stock purchases, employee ownership trusts, and others.

ESOPs that are structured as retirement plans also have the ability to borrow money in a tax effective way to move the ownership of a company to the next generation. These broad-based plans include all employees who qualify for participation. Individuals usually need to be with a company for at least one year, attain the age of 21, and be an employee on the last day of the company's fiscal year-end to receive shares. Shares are then allocated to employee owners based on their compensation including bonuses in relation to the total compensation of all employees. Regulations require that the company stock is valued every year and that the value be communicated to employees.

Employee stock ownership plans with a small "e" capture all other forms of employee ownership. These plans are less regulated and can be constructed in a number of ways. Though all plans will be memorialized by a legal document reflecting state laws, most rules revolve around the accounting by the sponsoring company.

DOI: 10.4324/9781003215417-4

Individuals receive or obtain this ownership through the board of directors of the sponsoring company that also dictates the terms of these plans. There is often no requirement for annual valuation.

Whether employee stock ownership plans are regulated or unregulated, they are a popular way of providing employees with an equity ownership stake in a business. By "stake" we mean a percentage share of a business's net worth, which is determined by its capital and profit (loss) history.

The possibility of a monetary gain or loss provides a direct incentive to employee owners to think and act like "owners" instead of just employees. By so doing, they should generally think and work harder to identify, and execute, profitable strategic initiatives. This is the theory behind employee ownership plans and, in general, it has proven to be the case in practice. For example, it has been estimated that businesses with employee ownership experience, on average, 4–5 percent more productivity than businesses without such programs. As a result, many employees have been able to create wealth from their participation in ownership plans over time.

One way to evaluate potential businesses to work for is to determine if they practice something called "open book management" (OBM). This managerial technique is designed to provide extreme levels of transparency to all employees through two interrelated initiatives. First, all employees are provided with all of the material information on a business and how it is run. Second, all employees are formally educated how to use the information that they will be receiving. The thought behind this initiative is that well-informed employees will be better able to contribute to successful business activities over time. This premise obviously makes a great deal of sense in theory and, importantly, it also works in practice.

According to a *Forbes* magazine article that was written by Bill Fotsch and John Case, "companies register as much as a 30 percent increase in productivity and profitability in the first year alone, when they implement the approach [OBM] properly."[1] Compare this increase with the productivity of companies that do not practice OBM, and what one finds is less employee engagement in the firms that do not share financial information with employees. While we do not have statistical proof for this next point, we believe that increased employee turnover comes about in businesses that do not practice OBM.

There are three broad tenets of open book management. First, every employee should develop and be given the information, including measures, of a business's success, *and* they should be taught how to understand and use them. As noted earlier, the managerial objective here is both complete business transparency *and* a broad base of informed users.

Second, armed with their knowledge and detailed business information, employees are both expected and enabled to use their skills and insights to improve the performance of the business over time.

And third, every employee should share in the profits and losses of the business via an ownership stake/ESOP. Taken together, all three tenets work together to increase overall productivity over time and, significantly, this occurs in extremely positive social environments.

In sum, OBM is a potent business practice that we believe will increasingly grow more popular. Businesses that consistently practice it are generally able to attract employees based both on the potential for wealth creation via an ESOP *and* the positive work environment in which the wealth is created.

Notice the word "potential" in the previous paragraph. Nothing in business is certain. To address the inescapable fact of economic uncertainty, most well-run businesses have corporate strategy functions. Strategy is also incredibly important in personal finance, but it is often overlooked. Therefore, we will profile both corporate strategy and personal finance strategy in the next chapter.

NOTE

1 Bill Fotsch and John Case, "The Business Case for Open-Book Management," *Forbes*, July 25 (2017), www.forbes.com/sites/fotschcase/2017/07/25/the-business-case-for-open-book-management/?sh=6f22474d5883

STRATEGY AND PRICES

To say that strategy is the darling of business school curriculums across the globe would be a gross understatement. There have literally been thousands of books and articles published on strategy over the years.[1] Despite all of this coverage, though, the basic definition of *strategy* is very straightforward: a plan or policy that is designed to achieve a desired end.

In business, successful strategies are known to have two core components: a value proposition that describes why customers will patronize a business, and a description of what differentiates a business from its competitors. While this may sound straightforward and easy to figure out, it is not, which is why truly successful strategies are so rare.

Instead of coming up with something truly unique, many businesses employ a "me too" strategy, which may strike some readers as odd given that differentiation was identified as a core tenet of a successful strategy. However, human beings are social animals, and therefore it is natural for many people in business to copy or track what their competitors are doing, especially if they are relatively successful. This behavior carries over to personal finance strategies with many people copying or benchmarking themselves against their "peer group," which typically includes friends, neighbors, co-workers, and family. Despite the widespread nature of this behavior, it is not advisable to use peer group or other social benchmarks to drive, inform, or influence your personal finance strategy.

Both of us stumbled upon the travails of peer group–based personal finance strategies early in our careers. For example, one of us was hired out of school into the insurance industry to adjust property

DOI: 10.4324/9781003215417-5

claims. The territory he covered included a very affluent town—by some measures the most affluent area in the United States—and his work required visits to several homes in this area. While people lived in all of the homes that were visited, some of the homes were barely furnished. When questioned about this, the people who lived in the relatively empty homes stated, in not so many words, that they could not afford furnishings. In other words, they were "house poor."

When one of these people was asked why they did not just live in a surrounding area that was more affordable, they pleasantly replied, "Oh my, how would that look?"

In addition to homes, luxury goods often form the basis of many personal finance benchmarks. While luxury goods are not needed to survive, they can make life easier for many people. For example, items like smart phones, tablets, and other kinds of technology have dramatically improved the quality of life for many people across the globe (including us). However, luxury-based spending can become a problem when either too many goods are purchased and/or too much is paid for the goods, which wastes money that could be spent on other, more important items and experiences.

Significantly, you can often only see the things that someone buys, not whether they made wasteful purchases or paid too much for their items. Also, just because someone has in their possession a variety of assets—or, in the words of the late, great comedian, George Carlin, "stuff"—that does not mean they own anything outright. With credit currently very easy to get (as of early-2021), many people go into debt to fund a variety of purchases, which can add up over time. This is one of the reasons why consumer debt levels are so high today.

Debt becomes a problem when it cannot be paid for, or "serviced," on a timely basis. People fall behind on their debt payments for a variety of reasons including the loss of a job, illness, a run of bad luck, or the simple fact that they can no longer afford to pay their bills because their spending habits "got away from them" over time.

There is a key strategic reason why you should not let social benchmarks drive, inform, or otherwise influence your spending decisions. No one knows your preferences, wants, or needs better than you do. Therefore, you—and you alone—should make all of the decisions pertaining to those preferences, wants, and needs over time. Whatever someone else may or may not buy or do is irrelevant to what you should buy or do. Therefore, to the extent that you feel under pressure to buy or do something because other people are buying or doing it, you should critically evaluate your motivations before you make a purchase.

BENJAMIN GRAHAM

Finance is a means to an end; it is not an end in and of itself. The "end" of personal finance is the lifestyle that it will fund. This seemingly obvious statement of fact is both extremely important and very often overlooked. For example, we are frequently approached by people we know, and asked questions about their potential investment strategies. We begin each conversation with the same question.

"What is the objective or activity that you're saving to fund?"

Invariably, the answer that we hear the most often is, "To make the most money possible."

"That is not what we mean," we reply trying to clarify. "What is the lifestyle that you're trying to fund?"

"The one where we make the most money possible."

After going round-and-round like this for a while, with people across all segments of the economy (lower income, middle income, and wealthy), we finally state, "What is the income level that you are targeting to fund your retirement, your children's education, etc.? That is what we want to know. Only then can we consider if the strategy that you're considering seems appropriate."

Remember, strategy—determining what you want to achieve and how to achieve it—always comes before finance and, in fact, all that personal finance is, is the way to fund a chosen lifestyle. Again, finance is *not* an end in itself. Perhaps the leading financial theorist and practitioner of all-time understood this better than anyone.

The late Benjamin Graham was the founder of modern securities (stock and bond) analysis. He is also the father of what has come to be known as "value investing." Graham is popularly known as the person who taught Warren Buffett how to invest in the popular course that he offered at Columbia Business School while Buffett was a student there. He was also Buffett's first employer out of business school. Clearly, if Graham could teach Buffett how to succeed at business and finance, he has something to teach us all.

In his memoirs, Graham observed how he quickly convinced himself that, "the true key to material happiness lay in a modest standard of living which could be achieved with little difficulty under almost all economic conditions."[2] Please read the preceding sentence again before continuing to the next sentence. What Graham is saying is that modest or conservative lifestyle strategies are easier to fund than aggressive or extravagant strategies, and that "ease" leads to both a generally happier and less stressful lifestyle over time. This is both a profound and historical truth, which frequently gets lost or forgotten in our modern, consumption-driven economy.

Graham goes on to state in his memoirs that he applied this strategy in two ways: First, he resolved, "never again to be maneuvered into ostentation, unnecessary luxury, or expenditures that I could not easily afford." In other words, he was not going to "follow the Joneses" or anyone else. Second, he developed skills outside of his investment management business to diversify his earnings power. Specifically, he wrote articles for the business and financial press of his day, and he acted as an expert witness in legal matters. We have followed Graham's example closely, which led to many unexpected career successes, including the opportunity to write this book.

Pricing is another area where we have closely followed Graham's advice, in both corporate and personal finance.

STRATEGY AND PRICES

Many economic commentators talk about "consumer prices." For example, there is often a great deal of discussion in the press about the *Consumer Price Index*, or CPI, which is a popular barometer of aggregate consumer prices. If you look at a long-term chart of the CPI it will show a generally increasing trend of prices since the year 1970.

While economic indices like the CPI can be useful for overview purposes, they tend not to be very practical because people do not always pay rising prices for the products and services that they buy. Some prices decline, like those for certain electronic devices, while other prices stay the same.

There are many different prices, but all prices generally fall within three main categories: discount prices, retail prices, and premium prices.

People pay *premium prices* when they purchase something that they very much desire, frequently in a hurry. For example, if a pipe bursts in your home and you call a plumber to immediately fix it, the price that he or she charges you will likely be higher than the price of a routine service call. A reason for the higher price could be that the plumber must "drop everything" to respond to your distress, which drives up his or her costs and therefore the price that he or she charges you. Or it may be that the plumber knows that he or she has you over a barrel and is therefore able to charge more.

Similarly, stores that do not have much competition can also charge their customers generally higher prices. For example, such stores may be serving a population that does not have easy access to transportation or other means to search out lower prices. Such circumstances practically forestall the search for better prices.

Another form of price is the *retail price*, which is the most common price and can be found in most grocery stores, department stores, restaurants, and at other merchants.

Discount prices, which are also known as wholesale prices, are price levels below—sometimes far below—retail prices. For example, discount prices can be found during or at store sales events, "going out of business sales," thrift shops, discount stores, tag sales, etc. In general, you should strive to pay discount prices whenever and wherever you can.

These descriptions are generally structured toward the prices that people pay for things, but the exact same logic applies to both buyers and sellers. For example, many people sell items to pawn shops. Pawn shops buy goods at discount prices, frequently heavily discounted prices, and then they sell those goods at retail prices.[3]

People sell to pawn shops for two main reasons: First, they do not want to take the time needed to sell their items at retail prices, and therefore they sell them to pawn shops at discount prices. Examples of this can be seen in the popular television show, *Pawn Stars*. A second reason people sell to pawn shops is that they need money in a hurry, and as such are willing to sell their items quickly at heavily discounted prices for ready cash.

Understanding the practical implications of the three kinds of prices can help you to become a better, more strategic buyer and seller. For example, because prices are based on both the perceived value of a good and how quickly people want the good, you will pay lower prices on average if you spend time "shopping around" for deals. In other words, instead of buying an item immediately at a retail price, delay the purchase and see if you can buy it later or somewhere else, at a discount price.

Occasionally, deals will arise in the retail space, so it is worth your time to look for them. For example, even though grocery stores, department stores, and restaurants tend not to negotiate on price, many will occasionally issue coupons or hold sales on select items. Therefore, taking time to "clip coupons," and to find out when sales are scheduled to be held, will help you to generally discount the prices that you pay over time.

The same approach can be used when you sell things. For example, instead of selling an item quickly to a buyer at a discount price, spend some time and try to find a retail buyer.

Time is money, so use your time to be more price conscious when both buying and selling. And make sure to keep a list of your price savings so that you can track how much money you've made by "buying low and selling high."

If you adopt a modest or conservative lifestyle, it will generally be easier and less stressful to fund over time. A key enabler of such a lifestyle is the purchase of goods and services at discount prices. Consistently doing this will help to swing the odds of long-term financial wellness in your favor. To increase these odds even more, you will need to proactively mitigate the risk of monetary loss, which is the subject that we turn to next.

NOTES

1 Joe is the author of the book, *Creating Strategic Value* (New York: Columbia Business School Publishing, 2020), and a contributing editor to the journal, *Strategy & Leadership*.

2 Benjamin Graham, *The Memoirs of the Dean of Wall Street* (New York, McGraw-Hill, 1996), p. 263.

3 Pawn shops also extend short-term, high cost, fully collateralized loans, which is a subject for another day.

RISK MANAGEMENT

Similar to what we saw with strategy in the last chapter, risk management is a popular subject both academically and practically in the world of business. Surprisingly, there is no one way to define "risk." As used here, *risk* means the possibility and amount of permanent financial loss. To appreciate what it takes to effectively manage risk over time, we will profile a master of corporate risk management, Andy Grove, who passed away on March 21, 2016.

By way of background, Andy Grove was the co-founder, former chairman and former CEO of the Intel Corporation, which is a company that makes very high-quality computer chips. Grove was also the author of one of our favorite business books, *Only the Paranoid Survive: How to Exploit the Crisis Points that Challenge Every Company* (New York: Currency, 1996). This book quickly became a business classic after it was published. It also has a great deal to teach about personal finance, personal investing, and career management.

Grove was known to be an intensely detail-oriented manager. He was also known for demanding that the people who worked for him also be detail-oriented. This has been a key driver of Intel's success over the years.

From a personal finance perspective, being detail-oriented means knowing exactly where and how your money is being spent each and every month. It also means understanding the interest rates and terms of the credit (mortgage, loans, and credit cards) that you may be using. Spending money wisely, and using credit conservatively, are absolute keystones of responsible corporate and personal finance.

From a personal investing perspective, being detail-oriented means monitoring and closely tracking the performance of the

DOI: 10.4324/9781003215417-6

people you have hired to manage your money. The wording of the prior sentence is very important: the people you have hired to manage your money *work for you*. You are their boss. Therefore, it is up to you to closely monitor and track their performance over time.

Grove's concept of "paranoia" also has important career risk management implications. Consider the following paragraph, which is taken from the preface of his book:

> The sad news is, nobody owes you a career. Your career is literally your business. You own it as a sole proprietor. You have one employee: yourself. You are in competition with millions of similar businesses: millions of other employees all over the world. You need to accept ownership of your career, your skills, and the timing of your moves. It is your responsibility to protect this personal business of yours from harm and to position it to benefit from changes in the environment. Nobody else can do that for you.

There are many people who have suffered, and who continue to suffer—both financially and psychologically—because they have not embraced the concept of "your career is literally your business." These people range from union workers who suffer from volatile hire-layoff-rehire cycles to older people who are laid-off toward the end of their "peak earnings" years (approximately the late 50s), as well as many other classes of employees.

A core theme of Grove's book is that "things change," and sometimes the changes are very big. Every big change has both winners and losers. Over time, "the winners" tend to be those who embrace change and find ways to make it work for them. Those waiting to be brought along by the change are at risk of being passed by and will suffer financially as a result. From a career risk management perspective, this means that everyone should have both a career development plan and a back-up plan.

Career development planning pertains to enhancing your technical or professional skill set, which is something that Benjamin Graham also preached, as we noted earlier in the last chapter. This can include taking select trade, technical (such as computer and software), and business courses (such as finance and accounting). If you cannot afford to pay for a course, ask your employer to pay for it.

Alternatively, many schools will allow you to audit a course either free of charge or for a minimal fee.

Regular coursework not only increases your knowledge base, but it also helps to increase your personal network. Networks are incredibly important when you are looking for a job or another career opportunity.

Having a career back-up plan entails outlining specific activities that you will undertake if you suddenly lose your job. Just about everyone, blue-collar and white-collar worker alike, should have a back-up plan because change *is* coming. It always has, and it always will. Andy Grove understood this, and he profited from it both professionally and personally, just like Benjamin Graham did, and just like we all can.

PERSONAL FINANCE AND GREED

People do not, of course, have to be "paranoid" like Andy Grove to be successful. However, a little paranoia can be a good thing, especially when it comes to mitigating the risks of greed. *Greed*—or the intense, self-absorbed desire for wealth, broadly defined—motivates behaviors that can generate extremely large personal finance risks. One example of such risks involves the infamous Bernie Madoff Ponzi scheme.

Both of us have had numerous conversations about Madoff's Ponzi scheme. One of the people that we spoke with was approached to invest with Madoff in the early 2000s, and he wisely refused. When we asked him why he refused to invest, he answered that, "It was long assumed that Madoff was 'doing something' illegal, likely 'front-running' (which is the practice of traders placing their own trades in front of their clients'). We don't do business with people like that."

When we pointed out that a great many successful and high-profile people invested with Madoff, our friend's response was both direct and insightful:

> Successful and high-profile people can be greedy just like everyone else. Many of them no-doubt thought that Madoff was a crook just like we did, but they mistakenly thought that he was "their" crook. In other words, they let their greed get the better of their judgment. Happens all of the time, unfortunately.

Later that evening, there was an episode of *American Greed* on television. In the episode, several elderly people were profiled who put all their retirement savings into a dubious investment that turned out to be fraudulent. We wondered why these people put everything they had into these investments, and then the television program provided an answer. One of the people who was profiled said something to the affect that, "I should have known better. I just got greedy."

It is natural to desire wealth. Who does not want nice things? However, many people assume that being wealthy means living a life of leisure and being worry-free. While this may be true for some wealthy people, it is most definitely *not* true for all of them. For example, we know several very successful professional investors. While each of these investors is very different personally, they have many things in common professionally. Foremost amongst these is their work ethic: these people, and their staffs, work a great deal more than 40 hours per week. Theirs is most definitely not a life of leisure.

Another thing that these investors have in common is an acute sense of risk. Investments can lose money for any number of reasons, and as such the professional investors that we know work very hard to identify and monitor all the potential causes of loss. In fact, some of them equate their long-term investment success with how intensely they worry about, and monitor, the risks of their investments.

Here are seven things that can be easily done to mitigate the risk of loss due to greed:

First, it is important to understand that you cannot be defrauded if you do not give your money to a fraudster. Therefore, you should always be extremely careful who you trust with your money.

Second, it is an indisputable fact that unethical people cannot be trusted. Period. Therefore, if you find yourself in an investment, or personal finance relationship, with a dubious or unethical person, you should end it.

Third, if you are presented with a seemingly "risk-free" investment opportunity, ask why you have been approached, or "targeted," with the opportunity. Generally, when a professional investor has a great idea, they will keep it to themselves to ensure that they maximize their profit.

Fourth, unless you have ample time to carefully screen potential investments, and to perform intensive due diligence on such opportunities—and by due diligence we mean a great deal more than simple Google searches—consider hiring a professional money management firm to invest for you.

Fifth, absent a very compelling reason, only hire large money management firms. Large firms tend to have large assets of their own and therefore ample amounts of insurance to protect those assets in the event of lawsuits.

Sixth, no matter who invests your money, you must carefully and continuously monitor their performance to ensure that things stay on track. If things veer off-track, you should take timely action to make corrections.

Seven, everyone has the potential to be greedy, which is why you must be careful not to let it get the better of your judgment. One way to accomplish this is to be vigilant about avoiding Ponzi Schemes.

PONZI SCHEMES

During the 1920s, the stock market was booming, and it seemed like money was "there for the taking." A man named Charles Ponzi certainly thought so. At the very start of the decade, he was working a fraudulent investment scheme that continues to bear his name. In recent times, the most famous "Ponzi Scheme" was conducted by Bernie Madoff, as discussed earlier. Madoff was arrested in 2008, and he passed away in prison on April 14, 2021.

Even though Ponzi schemes are well-known, their promised superior returns, which are frequently marketed with compelling financial narratives, consistently find victims. For example, an article published in early 2020 indicated that the value of Ponzi Schemes was the highest it has been in a decade,[1] which is a troubling trend.

Each Ponzi scheme can, and often does, affect numerous individuals. Significantly, Ponzi schemes are not the only form of financial fraud that can devastate personal savings. For example, the financial shenanigans that caused the failures of Enron and Worldcom in the early 2000s also devastated numerous individuals' savings.[2]

When evaluating an investment opportunity, the following considerations should be kept in mind to mitigate the risk of fraud in general, and the risk of Ponzi schemes in particular.

First, you should adopt the mindset of every successful professional investor that we know: radical skepticism. Frauds attract victims because the stories that fraudsters tell are very compelling. Therefore, if you start out—and remain—highly skeptical as you investigate an investment opportunity, you will mitigate the risk of being "sucked into" a fraudulent story. Once sucked into such a story, it can be very difficult to find your way out.

Second, you should find out why "you" have been presented— or targeted—with a particular investment opportunity. If you are not *wealthy*, which is formally defined as a net worth of more than $5 million, then you generally do not have money that you can comfortably afford to lose. Therefore, you should neither be approached to make a speculative investment nor should you participate in such investments.

The third consideration involves basic benchmarking. To understand what we mean by this, consider that Warren Buffett, the popular chairman and CEO of Berkshire Hathaway, is widely considered one of the most successful investors in history. Buffett posts all his shareholder letters online free of charge at: www.berkshire-hathaway.com/letters/letters.html. If you click on, for example, his 2014 letter, the first page that opens is a benchmarking page, which shows the annual percentage changes in Berkshire's net assets as well as data for the S&P 500, which is a popular stock market index.

If an investment opportunity that you are evaluating outperforms benchmarks like Berkshire Hathaway and the S&P 500, find out specifically why. If, while doing so, you come to feel that you have stumbled onto "the next Warren Buffett," then you should know that there is a greater chance of winning a Powerball lottery than there is of finding "the next Warren Buffett." Therefore, you should remain very skeptical.

If you get this far and still want to make an investment, then you should only invest a small amount of your money, so long as it can be comfortably lost. An absolute rule of personal finance is that you *never* put your home, livelihood, or all your savings at risk in any one investment. This is a "fail safe" in that if an investment fails, as many investments do, the loss you suffer will not be financially catastrophic.

If, after making an investment, you come to suspect that you may have been defrauded, our final consideration holds that you should immediately contact the authorities. The sooner you do so, the sooner you may be able to get your money back and bring the fraudster to justice. You have probably noticed that this is the same as commandment ten from Chapter 1. This is how strongly we feel about holding fraudsters accountable for their actions.

As we indicated earlier, Ponzi schemes unfortunately seem to be on the rise as of 2019. Now with the coronavirus pandemic and recession, more frauds could be uncovered. As it is often said, when the tide goes out, it is easier to see the trash. It is with this in mind that we will revisit the most famous Ponzi of them all, Bernie Madoff, and see what lessons his fraud holds.

MADOFF

Several years ago, we learned of a book that was written by victims of the Bernie Madoff Ponzi Scheme. It is titled, *The Club No One Wanted to Join: Madoff Victims in Their Own Words* (Andover, MA: Doukathsan Press, 2010), and it has much to teach about personal finance and investing.

Some of Madoff's victims were retirees who, after decades of thrift, had paid off the mortgages on their homes and were living comfortable lives. However, to increase the size of their investment portfolios, some re-mortgaged their homes to invest more of their money with Madoff. This is how one of the victim's explained their decision:

> In the spring of 2003, I had decided to renovate my small but comfortable Florida condo that was completely paid for; the advice given to me by my sage uncle and another financial advisor was to take a "little extra" out in a loan and move it over to Bernie. "Don't tie your money up in bricks and stones; have it out there working for you. You'll earn more with Bernie than the bank will charge you in interest." So, I did just that and started making monthly mortgage payments.

Needless to say, this was a very big mistake. It is also one of the reasons why our first commandment of financial wellness, which was profiled in Chapter 1, stated that your home is not a common investment; it is the place where you and your family live. Therefore, it should never be put needlessly at risk.

If someone advises you not to "tie your money up in bricks and stones; have it out there working for you" tell them that you do not want your home "working" anywhere. You want it right where it is, comfortably housing you and your family. Then, stop talking to the person because they are either too confident in whatever abilities they think that they may have, they do not know what they are talking about, or they are a fraudster, just like Bernie Madoff was.

Additionally, many of Madoff's victims had all their money under management with him. If just half of their money had been with another money manager, their savings would not have been completely lost. However, they were so confident in Madoff that they gave him all their money to invest.

There is a reason why fraudsters like Madoff are called "confidence men," or con men for short. For example, one of the things that all con men do is wrap themselves in respectability. Bernie Madoff was an absolute master of this in that he was a former chairman of the NASDAQ stock market. He was also investigated several times by the Securities and Exchange Commission (SEC) prior to his fraud collapsing and was cleared of potential wrongdoing each time. Furthermore, he was authorized by the Internal Revenue Service (IRS) to be an Individual Retirement Account (IRA) custodian. As such, many of his victims felt that the government effectively endorsed Madoff, which gave them comfort and confidence to give him all their money to manage. Understandably, they now feel betrayed.

It is important to understand that complying with governmental rules and regulations is "table stakes" in business. This means that all money managers must follow rules and regulations just to be, and remain, in business. Therefore, rule and regulation compliance is a minimum business and investment requirement. When an investment business meets these minimum requirements, it does not mean that the government has endorsed it. The implications of understanding the difference between meeting requirements and having an endorsement can be significant.

While you should obviously only do business with someone who is compliant with governmental rules and regulations, this does not mean that a compliant businessperson or money manager is either knowledgeable or even competent from an investment perspective. Therefore, abnormally good investment results, such as those reported for years by Madoff, must always be skeptically and thoroughly evaluated. If you lack the skills to do this, then you should not invest with the money manager, even if a "sage uncle" advises you to do so.

Managing risk is a very broad topic, and as a result we have covered a great deal of ground in this chapter. Rather than extend it further, we decided to end this chapter here, and to continue our discussion of risk in the next chapter; specifically, the risk of cyber fraud.

NOTES

1 Greg Iacurci, "Ponzi schemes Hit Highest Level in a Decade, Hinting Next 'Investor Massacre' May Be Near," *CNBC Markets*, February 11 (2020), www.cnbc.com/2020/02/11/ponzi-schemes-hit-the-highest-level-in-10-years.html

2 Howard Schilit wrote an excellent book on how to avoid financial schemes like this, which is appropriately titled, *Finance Shenanigans*, 2nd Ed. (New York: McGraw-Hill, 2002).

CYBER RISK

Society is becoming increasingly digital. While digitization brings many benefits, it also generates a number of cyber-related risks. For example, consider cyber-fraud.

As noted in Chapter 5, at the heart of virtually every fraud is a compelling narrative or story that profiles seemingly easy ways to make money. In reality, there is *no* easy way to create wealth. So, if someone tells you—or sends you an email—about a way to make "easy money," they are either a fraud or they do not know what they are talking about. Either way, you should neither talk to nor email such people. This is important because you cannot be defrauded if you do not give a fraudster your trust and, of course, your money.

A far more subtle cyber-crime is identity theft, which occurs when criminals obtain a victim's personal information, such as a birthdate and social security number, and then secure and use lines of credit in the victim's name.

There are three general ways that cyber-criminals steal personal information: (1) Directly from a victim via some form of con, (2) From a victim's computer via some form of program, and (3) From a website that houses a victim's information. Here are some ways to mitigate each of these risks.

First, make it a practice of never giving out either your birthdate or social security number. Exceptions to this rule are to your banks/ credit providers, insurance companies, and certain governmental agencies. Significantly, each of these entities are generally very careful with personal information and will not indiscriminately ask you

DOI: 10.4324/9781003215417-7

to provide it. Therefore, if you receive an email asking for this information that seems to be from any of these entities, you should first click on the email address to ensure that it is a "legitimate" address. By legitimate, we mean that the email address matches the entity in question. If it does not match, and many times in a fraudulent situation the addresses will not match, then you should permanently block the address and delete the email.

However, if the email address seems legitimate, you should still not respond to the email. Instead, call the local office of the entity in question and ask to speak with a manager to both confirm the request, and to clarify the reason for it.

Next, make it a point to never click on non-secure links in emails, especially in messages from people that you do not know. The reason to generally avoid email links is that some of them deploy programs designed to scan and retrieve personal information off a computer, which can be used to steal your identity, amongst other things. An example of a secure email link is a link found in a confirmation email that is sent after you have made an electronic purchase from a reputable merchant.

Despite suggestions like these, many computers will still be hacked, and much personal information will be stolen. Therefore, you should try not to have documents that contain personal information—such as tax returns, social security documents, and bank statements—on computers that are connected to the internet. Similarly, personal data should not be stored on portable flash drives, unless such drives are encrypted and carefully secured.

We understand that some of these suggestions may be difficult for some people to implement, but for others, the next recommendation could prove exceedingly difficult: do not list your birthday or provide many personal details about you and your family on social media. We know that a great many people enjoy social media, for whatever reasons, but it is in many ways a fraudsters' paradise. Therefore, at the very least, you should be very careful what you post and disclose on social media platforms.

You should also regularly monitor your credit history via subscription to a credit bureau such as TransUnion, Experian, or Equifax. If, while doing so, you come to suspect that credit lines in your name have been opened by someone else, you should immediately close the lines and have your credit history put on alert for fraudulent activity.

In sum, digital technology and the internet should be used with an appreciation of both the benefits of the experiences, as well as the risks emanating from cyber-land, which will likely continue to grow over time.

7

FINANCIAL STATEMENTS AND PERSONAL FINANCE

The prior chapters pertained to strategy, prices, and risk. In modern business, the discipline at the center of each of these areas is finance. And at the center of finance is accounting, which is also popularly known as "the language of business."

When many people hear the word "accounting" the first thing that invariably comes to their minds is the debits and credits of bookkeeping. While this discipline is very important to both corporate and personal finance, we will not profile basic bookkeeping in this book because it has been covered in numerous other outlets. Instead, we will profile the three basic financial statements of corporate finance and show how they can enable practical and successful personal finance practices.

There are three core financial statements that every business must prepare: (1) an income statement, which is also called the profit and loss statement, (2) a cash flow statement, and (3) a balance sheet. We will discuss each of these statements in turn and show how they practically relate to personal finance.

THE INCOME STATEMENT

The income statement is basically a list. It begins with the revenue or sales that a business generates, and then it lists the various expenses incurred in generating that revenue, including taxes. These amounts are subtracted from revenue to determine the amount of money that a business earned (or lost) over a given period (such as monthly, quarterly, or annually).

In a personal finance context, the income statement takes the form of a personal budget. A budget is also a list, and it begins with

DOI: 10.4324/9781003215417-8

a person's or family's annual salary, which is the personal finance equivalent of revenue. Then, subtracted from the salary, are all of the household's expenses, including taxes. Table 7.1 illustrates this concept via a simplified version of a sample household budget that is presented for illustration purposes only.

The table is set up as follows: the top line (a) is the salary. Coming next are a series of household expenses, lines (b) through (g), which are listed in descending order. The final items in our sample budget are donations and taxes on lines (h) through (j). Subtracting all the expenses, donations, and taxes from the salary results in a bottom-line, (k), of $500 that is available for savings.

As we indicated earlier, Table 7.1 is a simplified budget for illustration purposes only. A number of things on this budget are obviously missing, including medical insurance and medical expenses. The reason why we did not list expenses like these in our example is that medical insurance and expenses vary widely by household, and both can be extremely complicated. Adding complexity to a simple example like this detracts from the core discussion. Also, this is not a book that is focused on budgeting; rather, our objective is to demonstrate how a personal budget equates to an income statement, and to highlight some of the key personal finance takeaways.

Looking at Table 7.1, you will see that it represents a fairly "tight budget" in that only 1 percent of the salary ($500) is available to be saved, line (k), which does not leave much room for error if

Table 7.1 Simplified Annual Household Budget Example

Line		
(a)	$55,000	Salary or wages
(b)	$21,000	Mortgage at $1,750 per month
(c)	$5,200	Food at $100 per week
(d)	$3,600	Utilities at $300 per month
(e)	$3,300	Phone and internet at $275 per month
(f)	$2,400	Car payment at $200 month
(g)	$1,000	Clothes, shoes and miscellaneous
(h)	$5,000	Donations
(i)	$10,000	Income taxes
(j)	$3,000	Real estate and car taxes
(k)	**$500**	**Available for savings**

the listed expense amounts are exceeded. This "risk of exceedance" is why personal budgets should be watched closely, on a monthly basis, just like many business executives closely watch their income statements.

One area to focus on falls under line (g) in Table 7.1, "clothes, shoes and miscellaneous," especially the "miscellaneous" category that is intentionally broad. One item that often falls within categories like this is "luxury goods," but the purchase of such goods is obviously not reflected in the tight budget of this example.

The scope of luxury purchases is incredibly wide, even within a specific class of goods. For example, movie tickets, an album from iTunes, a smart phone, a tablet (such as an iPad), and a smart TV are all "luxury goods," which means that none of them is required to sustain a life.

Most people understandably want luxury goods, but many cannot afford to buy all the goods that they want. Therefore, some will purchase luxury goods "on time" using credit cards and store credit. For many people, such purchases have resulted in very large credit balances, which must be serviced on a timely basis. To understand the implications of this, we will "loosen" our budget from Table 7.1 a bit to reflect excess spending in luxury goods and present the results in Table 7.2.

As can be seen, line (g) in this revised budget has been increased to $4,000 from the $1,000 shown in Table 7.1. This level of spending

Table 7.2 Modified Annual Household Budget Example

Line		
(a)	$55,000	Salary or wages
(b)	$21,000	Mortgage at $1,750 per month
(c)	$5,200	Food at $100 per week
(d)	$3,600	Utilities at $300 per month
(e)	$3,300	Phone and internet at $275 per month
(f)	$2,400	Car payment at $200 month
(g)	*$4,000*	*Clothes, shoes and miscellaneous*
(h)	$5,000	Donations
(i)	$10,000	Income taxes
(j)	$3,000	Real estate and car taxes
(k)	**($2,500)**	**Debt needed to fund spending**

requires $2,500 in debt to fund it over this budgetary year as shown on the bottom line (k).

Significantly, annual budgets like the ones illustrated in our two tables are not prepared in a vacuum. For example, many of us likely know recent college graduates with five-to-six-figure credit card balances (in addition to large student loans), middle-aged blue-collar and white-collar workers alike living hand-to-mouth due to the amounts of household debt that they have accumulated, and elderly people who were forced to go back to work full-time, and/or move in with their children, so that they could pay off their large consumer debt obligations. Many situations like these have a common root cause: the purchase of goods—frequently luxury in nature—on credit that grew to unmanageable levels over time.

Sadly, despite the massive amounts of consumer debt that many people have accumulated, some have little or nothing to show for it. This is unfortunate, but it makes sense when you think about it. Luxury goods are temporary, and therefore such goods wear out over time. If they wear out before they have been paid off, people will find themselves paying interest on goods that they no longer use plus, of course, the cost of any replacement good that has been purchased.

One way to approach the purchase of luxury goods is through the corporate finance concept of "matching." Simply put, when well-run businesses buy things, they try to "match" the useful life of those things with the amount of time that is needed to pay for them. Buying luxury goods can be approached the same way. For example, if a good has a one-year life, then it should be fully paid for within one year. If it cannot be fully paid for within the year, then it simply should not be purchased.

Deferred purchases can then be added to another list that can be regularly reviewed for inclusion into future budgets, when matched funding is available. Such lists can include a wide range of information, which can be used to evaluate the tradeoffs of luxury goods. For example, the name of each good, an estimate of its useful life, the interest rate that will be paid once it is acquired if credit is used, retail prices, used prices from online discount outlets and local discount stores, and so on.

The process of preparing purchase evaluation criteria, such as that profiled here, is important because it helps to reduce the risk of "impulse buying." As discussed in Chapter 2, we are all familiar with the lengths to which many manufacturers will go to make their products desirable, and to make the purchase of those products seem urgent even when—especially when—it is not. Such marketing-generated pressures, as well as peer pressure to buy the latest "hot thing," have caused many people to financially over-extend themselves over time.

Having a budget and disciplined purchase evaluation criteria in-place prior to shopping has helped many people to resist the urge of impulse buying, and to defer the purchase of luxury goods that cannot be immediately paid for. These people were then able to allocate time and attention to paying down their existing credit balances and even, after a period of time, saving money for the proverbial "rainy day."

As the saying goes, "cash is king." This is especially true when people are under stress due to a job loss, illness, accident, or some other unfortunate event/series of events. Therefore, we will now turn our attention to the all-important cash flow statement.

THE CASH FLOW STATEMENT

Very simply, the cash flow statement profiles a business's cash outflows and its cash inflows over a given period of time (such as monthly, quarterly, or annually). The personal finance equivalent of the cash flow statement is the family checkbook in which payments, fees, and withdrawals (all of which are recorded as "debits" in the checkbook register) are written down and subtracted from deposits (or "credits" in the register) to give a monthly balance. This balance is the amount of cash that is available for payments or savings, and it should be easily reconciled with official bank statements on a monthly basis.

Cash is the lifeblood of finance—corporate and personal. There-fore, understanding how cash moves through both a business and a household is the key to responsible financial management. As easy as this is to do—in most cases, balancing a household checkbook takes less than one hour per month—many people simply do not do it. This is a very big mistake.

Most people work very hard for their money. Therefore, why not spend a little time to ensure that it is being spent wisely on things that you truly need? Balancing a checkbook monthly, and then comparing the outlays and balance to the household budget, is a great way to ensure that this is being done. Over time, such practices will result in higher amounts of personal "net worth," which is the subject that we will turn to next.

THE BALANCE SHEET

Calculating "net worth" is simplicity itself: you subtract what you owe from what you own; in other words, net worth equals your assets (what you own) minus your liabilities (what you owe). The standard way to visualize this is through a balance sheet.

Similar to our personal budget example, Table 7.3 is a simplified version of a personal balance sheet that is used for illustration purposes only. It is not a detailed description of a personal balance sheet.

The way to prepare a balance sheet is to list the most *liquid* assets first, which are the assets that can be most readily turned into cash. This is why "Cash" and the "Retirement Account" are listed first and second, respectively in Table 7.3 (although care is required here for if you liquidate a retirement account incorrectly, you can be required to pay extensive penalties). The same principle holds for liabilities: the shorter-term credit card debt on the righthand-side of the balance

Table 7.3 Sample Personal Balance Sheet

Assets		Liabilities	
Cash (including savings and checking accounts)	$750	Credit Cards	$2,000
Retirement Account (IRA, 401K, etc.)	$1,500	Car Loan	$4,800
Electronic Goods (cell phone, computer, tablet)	$1,500	Mortgage	$195,000
Furniture (including television)	$2,500		
Car	$5,000		
Home	$200,000		
Total	**$211,250**		**$201,800**
Personal Net Worth (Assets – Liabilities)			**$9,450**

Note: The $201,800 in total liabilities + $9,450 in personal net worth = $211,250, which is the amount of total assets. This is a fundamental accounting principle: total assets will always equal total liabilities + personal net worth.

sheet is listed first, then the longer-term car loan is listed followed by the very long-term home mortgage, which is recorded last.

Balance sheets are usually prepared based on *historical costs;* in other words, what has been paid for the assets that were acquired. In the case of this example, $5,000 was paid for a used car and $200,000 was paid for a home; therefore, both costs are recorded as the values of those assets on our sample balance sheet.

Historical cost is a good initial proxy for the value of an asset, but it is not "the" value. To understand why, consider that all physical goods wear out over time. As a result, the amount that is recorded for the electronic goods, furniture, and car in our example may overstate the value of those assets if they are old and worn out. Conversely, some assets can considerably appreciate over time such as a retirement account and a home, especially if they are on the right side of a powerful "bull market." That said, you should always start with historical costs and then conservatively work up (or down) from there as needed.

As you can see, the reason why there are three different financial statements is because each statement records and tracks a different aspect of financial activity. The personal budget (income statement) lists what you make and what you spend, the cash flow statement (checkbook) records the cash implications of your salary and spending, and the balance sheet lists what you own (and owe) and therefore reflects the cumulative impact of your economic activity.

To demonstrate the practical implications of the statements to personal finance, we will project our illustrative balance sheet example out three or so years into the future. In doing so, we will hold all our values constant except the liabilities: mortgage debt and the car loan will be reduced over the years as we reasonably assume that regular loan and mortgage payments have been made, thereby reducing the principal. This is a positive development, but the amount of credit card debt in our example is being increased to $20,000. Significantly, this increase did not occur all at once: there was a costly vacation one year, some luxury goods purchased the following year, expensive presents purchased in all the years, then another costly vacation in the last year, but it all adds up as shown in Table 7.4.

As can be seen, the added credit card debt has far out-weighed the principal reductions in the car and mortgage loans, and therefore resulted in a negative net worth of -$350. Significantly, this

Table 7.4 Modified Sample Personal Balance Sheet

Assets		Liabilities	
Cash (including savings and checking accounts)	$750	*Credit Cards*	*$20,000*
Retirement Account (IRA, 401K, etc.)	$1,500	*Car Loan*	*$1,600*
Electronic Goods (cell phone, computer, tablet)	$1,500	*Mortgage*	*$190,000*
Furniture (including television)	$2,500		
Car	$5,000		
Home	$200,000		
Total	**$211,250**		**$211,600**
Personal Net Worth (Assets – Liabilities)			**($350)**

added debt does not reflect the added burden of the high interest rates that many credit cards charge. Such rates make it very difficult to pay down/off debt when credit balances grow large. Further, it is difficult for some people to stop excessive spending once they have started. You can see how a problem like this can spiral out of control.

There is a way to gain perspective in areas like this, and it combines elements of strategy, which we covered in Chapter 4, along with the largest asset that most people will ever own—their home. This is the subject that we will address in Chapter 9. First, though, we will extend our discussion of financial statements into the next chapter; specifically, as it pertains to small business finance.

8

SMALL BUSINESS FINANCE

According to a study conducted by author Georgia McIntyre, nearly 30 percent of small businesses fail because they run out of cash, and an additional 18 percent fail due to pricing and cost issues.[1] In other words, almost half of all small business failures are due to issues that trace directly to one of the three financial statements, especially the cash flow statement (personal checkbook) and income statement (personal budget). These are remarkable statistics, which match what we have observed in practice.

We will start this chapter with a discussion of cost issues. In Chapter 4 we mentioned Benjamin Graham who is the late founder of "value investing," and the man who taught Warren Buffett how to invest at Columbia Business School. The core of Graham's approach is economical buying, which means striving to pay wholesale rather than retail prices whenever and wherever possible. Despite the inherent logic of this approach, it is not often followed, which can cause financial distress to both businesses and people. This is particularly applicable to small business owners who, in our opinion, should all be habitually frugal buyers.

There can be a fine line between being frugal and being "cheap." It is usually not good practice for a business owner to be "cheap" because you will generally get what you pay for over time. In contrast, it is always good to be a frugal buyer by taking advantage of sales, discounts, and other tactics we discussed in Chapter 4 to limit the prices that you pay on the goods your business requires over time.

We now turn to pricing issues. In many ways, pricing is the converse of cost, but more importantly, it is one of the two key factors that determine how much revenue a business generates (the other

DOI: 10.4324/9781003215417-9

factor is the amount or quantity of goods or services sold as revenue equals price times quantity).

What should you price for a good or service? This is a simple but complicated question, which can generally be answered in one of three ways. The first pertains to how your expected price will compare to the average market price of similar goods and services offered by your competitors. The successful small business owners that we know intensely track the prices of both their marketplaces and each of their competitors, almost to the point of obsession. Such intense focus enables them to remain both price competitive and profitable across their respective business cycles.

The second way to price a good or service is via something known as "cost-plus," which involves calculating the unit cost of each good or service and then adding some margin to that cost to hopefully create a profit. Needless to say, this approach requires a very detailed and continuous understanding of the business's costs, which a comprehensive income or profit-and-loss statement will provide.

A third way to establish a price is via some ad hoc method. For example, an interior designer we know initially priced her services to be competitive in her local marketplace. However, her business was not doing well, despite all of the extra services she was providing. As a result, she dramatically *increased* the prices that she was charging. She felt that by doing this she would signal her premium services to her targeted client base. And, along with an effective marketing campaign, that is exactly what occurred.

In practice, prices are frequently established using all three of these methods in tandem. Regardless of the method chosen, however, all of the successful small business owners we know rigorously track the revenue and costs their businesses generate on at least a monthly basis (and frequently on a weekly basis) via basic income statement analysis.

These owners also closely watch the cash coming in and going out of their businesses, and they take care to ensure that their cash holdings will not run dry. They do this by formulating contingency plans beforehand, which could entail opening a line of credit with a bank before the use of credit is needed, negotiating trade credit agreements with suppliers before such credit is needed, and identifying other potential sources of credit (such as governmental loans) that could be approached if the need arises. The key here is to closely track the inflow and outflow of cash via the cash flow statement, and to then take precautions to ensure that cashflow does not disappear during temporary bouts of economic volatility by securing financing options before they are needed, which are recorded on the righthand-side of a balance sheet.

It is not an accident that nearly 50 percent of small business failures are caused by financial issues. While financial statement expertise alone will not ensure a successful small business, it will go a very long way in helping to ensure that a successful small business remains successful over time.

Remember, also, what we said in Chapter 3. Open book management can be an important part of business success. Not only do open book management and employee ownership help workers, they can be good for small business owners as well. When employees understand the finances of a company, they are better able to service customers, make decisions that are within their purview, and help a business grow.

But to use open book management in your business, you have to keep accurate and up to date books that are easy to understand.

NOTE

1   Georgia McIntyre, "What Percentage of Small Businesses Fail? (And Other Need-to-Know Stats)." *Fundera*, November 20 (2020), www.fundera.com/blog/what-percentage-of-small-businesses-fail#:~:text=What%20Is%20the%20Small%20Business,their%2010th%20year%20in%20business

9

YOUR HOME

In Chapter 4 we talked about strategy. We also discussed the late Benjamin Graham, and how he felt that "the true key to material happiness lay in a modest standard of living which could be achieved with little difficulty under almost all economic conditions." The word "modest" in the last sentence should not be read pejoratively. It should also not be read to imply "substandard living." Many people live comfortable and happy lifestyles that they can easily fund. That is the meaning of modest, and it is a worthy goal for us all.

At the center of everyone's lifestyle is their home. For many people, their home is also the largest asset that they will ever buy. We saw this in the personal balance sheet example profiled in the Chapter 7, which is reproduced in Table 9.1.

As Table 9.1 shows, the home in this example cost $200,000. Given this cost, the purchase required financing over time via a mortgage. Mortgages are expensive, which we also saw in the personal budget example in Chapter 7, and which is reproduced in Table 9.2 that shows a monthly mortgage expense of $1,750 in line (b).

How great would it be to live without a mortgage, and the expense of servicing it, every month? Most people would likely answer this question, "It would be absolutely GREAT!" Nevertheless, relatively few people plan or work toward being mortgage free anymore. This was not always the case.

MORTGAGE BURNING PARTIES

One of us recently had dinner with three friends. Of the three, one seemed to be in particularly good spirits. When we asked him why,

DOI: 10.4324/9781003215417-10

Table 9.1 Modified Sample Personal Balance Sheet

Assets		Liabilities	
Cash (including savings and checking accounts)	$750	Credit Cards	$20,000
Retirement Account (IRA, 401K, etc.)	$1,500	Car Loan	$1,600
Electronic Goods (cell phone, computer, tablet)	$1,500	Mortgage	$190,000
Furniture (including television)	$2,500		
Car	$5,000		
Home	$200,000		
Total	**$211,250**		**$211,600**
Personal Net Worth (Assets – Liabilities)			**($350)**

Table 9.2 Modified Annual Household Budget Example

Line		
(a)	$55,000	Salary or wages
(b)	*$21,000*	*Mortgage at $1,750 per month*
(c)	$5,200	Food at $100 per week
(d)	$3,600	Utilities at $300 per month
(e)	$3,300	Phone and internet at $275 per month
(f)	$2,400	Car payment at $200 month
(g)	$4,000	Clothes, shoes and miscellaneous
(h)	$5,000	Donations
(i)	$10,000	Income taxes
(j)	$3,000	Real estate and car taxes
(k)	**($2,500)**	**Debt needed to fund spending**

he stated that he had just paid off his mortgage. Before we could congratulate him, one of our other friends asked him, "What fun is there in that?"

When we asked this person what he meant by "fun," he responded that because no-one knows what tomorrow will bring, we should all live life to the fullest today regardless of the cost. Upon hearing this, we noted that, amongst other things, a "live life to the fullest today" approach could lead to serious financial problems. Furthermore, we observed that,

While we can never know "what tomorrow will bring," we do know that the average life expectancy in the United States is roughly the late-70s. We also "know" that the average person's *peak earning years*, or the years someone is expected to make their highest salaries, is generally between their mid-40s to mid-50s. This leaves roughly 20 years between the end of peak earnings and the average life expectancy. Therefore, if your mortgage and other debts are not paid off before then how will you finance them?

Our question was a loaded one because several of our other friends, who are all in their 50s, have lost their jobs and are currently struggling to service their debts, and pay their bills. In fact, we have seen so many cases like this—from both white-collar and blue-collar workers alike—that it was one of our motivations to write this book.

A couple of generations ago people like our grandparents held "mortgage burning parties," which literally involved burning all of one's loan documents once a mortgage is paid off. This act was viewed as an important rite of passage: owning a home outright. It was also viewed as an integral part of the American Dream. Somehow this rite of passage and dream has unfortunately been lost. We would do well to get it back.

By mortgage burning parties we do not mean that you should literally burn all of your mortgage documents once a home is paid off. For example, the mortgage satisfaction document should be kept for legal purposes. But many of the standard mortgage documents can indeed be "burned" once a mortgage has been completely paid off.

As we have stated before, your home is where you and your family live. It is not an investment with equity to "unlock" or an ATM-like repository of cash to "extract." This does not mean that a home is not an "investment," but it does mean that it is a very special kind of investment: one that will enable you and your family to be housed relatively "free" once it is completely paid for. By "relatively" free we mean that the costs of utilities, maintenance expenses and, of course, taxes will still have to be paid when a mortgage is paid off.

However, relatively free living can dramatically transform one's personal finances. To understand what we mean, we will delete the mortgage payment from our personal budget example in Table 9.2, and then we will recalculate the result in Table 9.3. This scenario is obviously an oversimplification because we held the salary and all other expenses, as well as the taxes, flat which likely would not occur in practice. Nevertheless, the calculated result is highly illustrative: $18,500 is now available for savings (line (k)) instead of the $2,500 deficit shown in Table 9.2.

Incredibly, the impact of a fully funded home on a person's net worth is even more dramatic. To see how, we will delete the mortgage liability from our personal balance sheet example in Table 9.1, and then we will recalculate the result in Table 9.4.

Table 9.3 Modified Annual Household Budget Example—No Mortgage

Line		
(a)	$55,000	Salary or wages
(b)	*$0*	*Mortgage—house paid off*
(c)	$5,200	Food at $100 per week
(d)	$3,600	Utilities at $300 per month
(e)	$3,300	Phone and internet at $275 per month
(f)	$2,400	Car payment at $200 month
(g)	$4,000	Clothes, shoes and miscellaneous
(h)	$5,000	Donations
(i)	$10,000	Income taxes
(j)	$3,000	Real estate and car taxes
(k)	**$18,500**	**Available for savings**

Table 9.4 Modified Sample Personal Balance Sheet—No Mortgage

Assets		Liabilities	
Cash (including savings and checking accounts)	$750	Credit Cards	$20,000
Retirement Account (IRA, 401K, etc.)	$1,500	Car Loan	$1,600
Electronic Goods (cell phone, computer, tablet)	$1,500	*Mortgage*	*$0*
Furniture (including television)	$2,500		
Car	$5,000		
Home	$200,000		
Total	**$211,250**		**$21,600**
Personal Net Worth (Assets – Liabilities)			**$189,650**

This table is also a simplified example in that it also holds all the other values constant, which likely would not often occur in practice. Nevertheless, the result is illustratively striking: an increase in net worth from -$350 to $189,650. Clearly, paying off a mortgage is a worthy personal finance goal.

There are several ways to pay off a mortgage. The first entails making the required payments every month for the duration of the loan, which is usually 20 to 30 years. That is a very long time, but if you do not use your home as collateral for other loans (such as home equity loans), it is the basic way to pay off a mortgage.

If you have disposable income, and there is no penalty for pre-paying your mortgage, then you can make extra payments to pay off a mortgage much faster. For example, if you make one extra mortgage payment a year on a typical 30-year fixed rate mortgage, you can reduce your mortgage duration by approximately 8 years (for example, to 22 years from 30 years).

Admittedly, this may not sound like "fun" to some people, which is why we should bring mortgage burning parties back. Parties are fun, and there are not very many things better to celebrate than being mortgage free. Of course, financial discipline is still required once a mortgage has been paid off, and in some cases, it may be more important.

For example, in Chapter 5 we noted that some of the people who were defrauded by Bernie Madoff had re-mortgaged their homes to increase the size of their investment portfolio with him. It was obviously a mistake to invest with Madoff, but more generally it is almost always a mistake to re-mortgage a home. Remember, your home is where you and your family live. It is not a financial asset to play with regardless of what anyone may tell you, and that includes politicians and economists. It is important to specify this because, at times, politicians and economists have given erroneous advice in areas like this.

For instance, in July of 2001, Alan Greenspan was the chairman of the Federal Reserve, which is the United States' central bank. Greenspan commented favorably at that time about how American homeowners were using their homes as collateral to fund their purchasing activity. He was absolutely incorrect in praising this, and so is anyone else who says similar things regardless of their official rank or celebrity.

REVERSE MORTGAGES

In our examples, we illustrated the financial benefits of paying off a mortgage by way of illustrative personal budget and personal balance sheet scenarios. In our scenarios, we held everything constant except for the mortgage and its monthly expense. However, and as we all know, over time *everything* changes.

If a person has not saved enough money for the time when they are no longer able to work full-time, or even part-time, then they will likely find that they will no longer be able to pay the expenses and taxes associated with a paid-off home. What happens then?

Some people in situations like this have turned to a "reverse mortgage," which is a topic that has received a great deal of publicity, often via media personality spokespeople or pitchmen who endorse the product. Significantly, it is doubtful that these spokespeople either understand technical finance or would ever find themselves in a situation that required them to reverse mortgage their homes.

By way of background, a *reverse mortgage* is basically a financial product that allows certain senior homeowners to borrow money using their homes as collateral. Significantly, this money does not have to be paid back until the borrower either passes away, moves, or sells their home. In other words, there are no monthly mortgage payments involved. This deferred payment feature is the main attraction of a reverse mortgage.

A number of people have been attracted to reverse mortgages in the belief that such mortgages were "the answer" to their personal finance problems. However, some of these people have come to regret their decision to obtain a reverse mortgage.

Two main questions must be answered when evaluating a reverse mortgage. First, is enough money being offered by way of a reserve mortgage? And second, how will the money be used? Each of these questions is considered in the following paragraphs.

Many people are familiar with the mechanics of a traditional mortgage. For a fixed timeframe (such as 20 or 30 years), money is borrowed at a given interest rate based on the collateral of the home being purchased. What happens in a reverse mortgage?

A reverse mortgage is valued based on several factors such as interest rates, life expectancies, home values, and a "margin" for the bank that is reversing or "discounting" the mortgage. The mechanics of discounting are not complicated for people with financial training, but for those without such training it can seem a bit like a foreign language. And, as with any language, if you are not conversant in it, you likely will not understand what is being said.[1] This is important because you should never contractually agree to anything that you do not thoroughly understand, and that includes a reverse mortgage. If you do not understand exactly how the money you are receiving in a reverse mortgage was calculated and are therefore unable to estimate if it is a fair amount, then you should not consider such a mortgage.

The second question pertains to how money from a reverse mortgage will be used or spent. This is important because the people who are considering a reverse mortgage are obviously financially constrained: why else would they be considering such a mortgage?

If the money that is received from a reverse mortgage is not enough for the rest of a borrower's life, they could face further—and perhaps even more intensive—financial constraints when the money runs out. Sadly, this is what has happened to some of the people that we know who reverse-mortgaged their homes.

When we spoke to some of these people before they had reverse mortgaged their homes, it was glaringly apparent that they were simply no longer able to comfortably afford the homes that they were living in. After questioning them on this, they replied, "We really don't want to move. We love it here."

Our response was that the question they needed to address what not what they may or may not "want," but rather, what they can comfortably afford. We asked, "If you reverse mortgage your home and then use the money to live on, it may run out given your expense base. What will you do then?"

It is crucial to ask and answer tough questions like these because, amongst other things, if reverse mortgage borrowers are unable to pay a property's maintenance expenses, taxes, and insurance, they could be found in default of the reverse mortgage's terms. Defaulting on a reverse mortgage has consequences, including the possible loss of one's home.

For many people, scaling down to a more affordable home can be a much better financial option to explore than a reverse mortgage. Remember, the strategy of sound personal finance is to comfortably fund a chosen lifestyle. A home that cannot be comfortably afforded is not consistent with this strategy. Therefore, the sale of such homes should at least be evaluated, along with some of the contents that have been accumulated over time.

The costs of smaller, more readily affordable homes can then be considered. Smaller homes generally come with smaller tax bills, smaller insurance costs, smaller utility expenses, and smaller maintenance expenses. Therefore, "living smaller" could also mean "living better," which does not always happen with a reverse mortgage.

Regardless of the option that may be chosen—reverse mortgage or the sale of a more expensive home—the strategic objective should be to make your lifestyle comfortable and easier to afford. An effective way to accomplish this over time is to use debt sparingly, if at all, especially as you age. This is the topic that we turn to in the next chapter.

NOTE

1 Virtually all introductory finance books cover the mechanics of present value and discounting. For an example see, Ehsan Nikbakht and A.A. Groppelli, *Finance*, 6th Ed. (New York: Barron's, 2012 [1986]).

10

BE CAREFUL WITH DEBT

An article was published in *Time* magazine several years ago that generated a great deal of attention. It was titled, "The United States of Insolvency," and it was written by James Grant who is a noted financial analyst, journalist, and historian, as well as a friend of ours. Here is how the article begins: "This much I have learned about debt after 40 years of writing and study: It is better not to incur it. Once it is incurred, it is better to pay it off. America, we have a problem."[1]

The article goes on to profile the extreme spending undertaken by the United States government, which at the time of the article had resulted in nearly $14 trillion of national debt. To put this number into context: $14 trillion = $14 million x 1 million. At the time of this writing, the national debt is incredibly, and sadly, double that amount at $28.1 trillion.[2]

Our national financial position reflects individual spending habits. One of us witnessed an example of this shortly after Mr. Grant's article was published. At the time, we were at a dinner party and were somewhat surprised to see that our hosts had completely renovated their kitchen. We were surprised as both the husband-and-wife hosts had been out of work for months.

The kitchen was beautifully done, but its timing seemed risky to us. When we discretely asked about this, the hosts responded, "We really wanted a new kitchen, and with financing rates so low we just went ahead and did it!"

We readily concede that financing rates were indeed low at the time and are also low at the time of this writing, but monthly loan payments still must be made. And without family paychecks,

DOI: 10.4324/9781003215417-11

absent a very large bank account, it could be difficult to make such payments.

A common reply to statements pointing these facts out is, "We lived with our old kitchen for such a long time and have always made our mortgage payments, so we deserve this!" People who feel this way are effectively saying that they feel entitled to a renovation that they cannot afford.

As Mr. Grant noted in his article, one of the ways that the government manages its finances is by paying its bills with money that it creates or "prints." We cannot print money. If we do, we will go to jail for counterfeiting. Therefore, we must pay our bills when they are due with money that we earn or we risk losing the things that we purchased with credit, including our homes.

The hosts who we described here were in their late-50s, and when we politely questioned them further on their use of debt, they said that their "worst case scenario" was that they would use their forthcoming Social Security checks to pay their bills. When we asked what they would do if the government deferred or reduced Social Security benefits, they answered, "They can't do that!"

Well, "they" certainly can do that, and indeed "they" will eventually have to do something like that as our national debt is not going to stop growing until we start paying it down and reduce our spending. At some point in the future—no-one knows when, of course—this will occur. It simply has to, or the economy could collapse.

Government entitlement programs like Social Security were originally designed as financial backstops. However, over time the politicians of both parties expanded the scope of the programs to attract voters. This is what most politicians have done across time, and what they continue to do today.

The takeaway here is that your personal finance decisions should not be based on political promises, especially if you are at or near retirement age. Rather, luxury-based spending should be controlled so that any debt you have can be paid down, and preferably off, prior to your retirement or when you are only working part-time. The same holds true for your home, as we discussed in the last chapter. If you cannot comfortably afford to live in it anymore, consider selling it and moving into a smaller or more comfortably affordable home.

We realize that this flies in the face of the instant gratification consumerism that many people have unfortunately grown accustomed to. However, Mr. Grant was correct in that it is better not to incur debt or, if it is incurred, to pay it off. Doing so will likely prevent you from buying at least some of the things that you may feel you "deserve." But you will also avoid the stresses brought on by financial pressures, which, by avoiding, will help to make your older years truly "golden."

If you choose to use debt (or credit), it is critically important that you understand the terms associated with it, and this means that you must read and understand the "fine print" of your credit documents.

THE FINE PRINT

Following a newspaper column that we wrote several years ago on consumer debt, we had the opportunity to discuss the subject with several people. One of the questions that we were asked was particularly enlightening, "In addition to scaling back spending, what else can someone do to better manage their use of credit?"

Our answer was, just as we stated earlier, that they should read all the terms and conditions of their credit agreements, especially those pertaining to interest rate resets.

As the conversation continued someone asked, "By credit agreements do you mean all of the papers that I was sent with my credit card? The ones with all of the small print that is hard to see?"

That is exactly what we mean. You need to read the fine print on all legal documents, including and especially credit agreements.

Our friends told us later that when they went home and were able to review their credit documents, they saw things like, "zero percent interest for the first year." After that, the rate resets to a very high interest rate, in some cases as high as 18 to 25 percent.

We were then asked, "How is this possible? With interest rates at such low levels, I just assumed that my interest rate would also be low."

We empathize when we hear things like this, but a central rule of finance—corporate and personal—is that you must be very careful when making assumptions. And you only make one after you have read and thoroughly understand everything, especially the fine print.

Just because interest rates in general are low does not mean that your particular interest rate will also be low. Credit providers, as well as other financial institutions like insurance companies, frequently offer low "teaser rates" because they know that such rates will attract customers. They also know that most customers will not read their credit or other financial agreements, especially the fine print, and as a result these customers will not react when their teaser rates are reset at higher, less appealing rates.

One way to manage the risk of things like this happening is to keep a running list of your credit lines. The list could include recording information such as: (1) the name of each credit provider, (2) the date each account was opened, (3) the amount of each credit line, (4) initial interest rate levels, (5) reset provisions/rates, (6) the current interest rate, (7) late payment penalty provisions, etc.

With information like this you can do a variety of things to better manage your use of credit. For example, prior to any reset you can call your credit provider and let them know that you are considering closing the account if the "teaser rate" is not continued, or unless some other accommodation is made. Alternatively, you can simply take advantage of other low teaser rates by rolling over credit balances prior to any scheduled reset.

A word of caution here: a key assumption with strategies like these is that your credit balances can be refinanced at rates that are lower than impending reset rates. Such assumptions have generally been valid since the early 1980s due to generally declining interest rates since that time. However, a growing number of successful professional investors are cautioning that the downward trend in interest rates is at risk of reversing. Like all prices, interest rates can go up as well as down, as indeed they have in the past.[3]

If interest rates in general do begin to move higher, implementing credit strategies like those profiled here will become increasingly difficult. Therefore, such strategies should be used only as part of a program to manage credit balances down over time. They should not be used to fund increased levels of discretionary spending, especially luxury-based spending.

NOTES

1 Here is a link to the article at *Time* magazine, https://time.com/4293549/james-grant-united-states-debt/

2 Here is a link to the U.S. Debt Clock, https://usdebtclock.org/

3 The seminal book on this subject is, Sidney Homer and Richard Sylla, *A History of Interest Rates,* 4th Ed. (Hoboken, NJ: Wiley, 2005 [1963]).

11

PHYSICAL AND
FINANCIAL WELLNESS

We have talked a great deal in this book about setting easy-to-achieve financial goals that can be comfortably afforded. Being financially comfortable is important because it greatly reduces stress levels. And as we have also mentioned, stress can lead to a variety of illnesses, and even death in some cases.

A friend recently forwarded us an article that profiled the following statistics from a popular survey:

- 70 percent of adults in the United States said that they care more about their physical health than their financial health—thereby ignoring the all-important link between the two.
- 49 percent of men, and 38 percent of women, said that they care more about how much they weigh, than how much debt they carry.
- 72 percent of Americans said that they would prefer to keep their current amount of debt, rather than increase their weight by 25 pounds and be debt-free.

The trade-off between physical health and financial wellness is obviously a false one. People can be both physically healthy and financially healthy. They can also be both physically ill and financially ill. More important is the fact that financial health can influence physical health, and vice versa. For example, a physically healthy person can become sick due to financial distress, which we have unfortunately observed numerous times. Similarly, someone who is physically ill could become healthy following a relaxing vacation that they can easily afford.

How, then, should we think about this survey and its odd statistics? It is important to first put them into context. An article by

DOI: 10.4324/9781003215417-12

American Banker noted that, in 2018, household debt hit another all-time high. Such debt has increased every year since 2012.[1] Now, we concede that trends like these are very difficult to chart and accurately analyze, and therefore we use them only to illustrate our core point: Consistently higher levels of debt are being used to fund lifestyle choices in the United States, some of which will likely prevent the debt holders from being financially comfortable as they age. Again, it is critically important to appreciate how often financial wellness can influence physical wellness.

While financial wellness is admittedly a broad topic, it can be practically assessed along the following three dimensions:

1 The difference between how much a person owns and how much they owe (the personal balance sheet that we profiled in Chapter 7)
2 The amount of fixed and discretionary expenses that are funded by one's salary, retirement funds or other earnings (the personal budget)
3 The amount of savings that are set aside for a "rainy day" and retirement

We will consider each of these dimensions in turn. First, consider the difference between how much a person owns and how much they owe, which is particularly important with respect to property such as homes and automobiles. A common financial measure for this is the *Loan-to-Value (LTV) ratio*, which compares the current amount of a loan to the value of the property securing (or collateralizing) it. A low LTV ratio is a sign of strong financial health.

To demonstrate how the LTV ratio works, we will revisit our personal balance sheet example from Chapter 7. First, we will profile a high LTV personal balance sheet from that chapter in Table 11.1. The calculations shown in **bold** font in the table reflect a high LTV ratio of 93.5 percent (= [$190,000 mortgage + $1,600 car loan] / [$200,000 home value + $5,000 car value]).

Next, we will profile the low LTV personal balance sheet that is also from Chapter 7 where the calculations are again in **bold** font. These calculations reflect a very low LTV ratio of 0.8 percent (= [$0 mortgage + $1,600 car loan] / [$200,000 home value + $5,000 car value]). As you can see from Table 11.2, this ratio reflects a very

Table 11.1 Modified Sample Personal Balance Sheet

Assets		Liabilities	
Cash (including savings and checking accounts)	$750	Credit Cards	$20,000
Retirement Account (IRA, 401K, etc.)	$1,500	Car Loan	$1,600
Electronic Goods (cell phone, computer, tablet)	$1,500	Mortgage	$190,000
Furniture (including television)	$2,500		
Car	$5,000		
Home	$200,000		
Total	$211,250		$211,600
Personal Net Worth (Assets – Liabilities)			($350)
Loan-to-Value Ratio: Car + Home	**93.5%**		

Table 11.2 Modified Sample Personal Balance Sheet—No Mortgage

Assets		Liabilities	
Cash (including savings and checking accounts)	$750	Credit Cards	$20,000
Retirement Account (IRA, 401K, etc.)	$1,500	Car Loan	$1,600
Electronic Goods (cell phone, computer, tablet)	$1,500	Mortgage	$0
Furniture (including television)	$2,500		
Car	$5,000		
Home	$200,000		
Total	$211,250		$21,600
Personal Net Worth (Assets – Liabilities)			$189,650
Loan-to-Value Ratio: Car + Home	**0.8%**		

strong personal finance position, which can equate to higher levels of wellness over time.

We will now move on to fixed monthly expenses (such as rent/mortgage payments, food, utilities, etc.) and discretionary monthly expenses (such as cell phones, cable television, restaurants, etc.). These expenses can be compared to monthly earnings to calculate an *expense ratio*. As with the LTV ratio, a stronger (which in this case means lower) expense ratio is a sign of strong financial health.

To demonstrate how the expense ratio works, we will revisit our personal budget example from Chapter 7. First, we will profile a high expense ratio personal budget in Table 11.3. The calculations are shown in **bold** font and reflect a high expense ratio of 70 percent.

Next, we will profile the low expense ratio personal budget from Chapter 7. The calculations are once again in **bold** font in Table 11.4 and reflect a 32 percent expense ratio. As you can see, a lower expense ratio like this reflects a stronger annual personal finance position, which often equates to lower levels of shorter-term financial stress over time.

We want to share a word on ratio usage in general before we move on. While ratios are useful measures, as the previous examples illustrate, that is all they are: measures. Ratios are not the "end" of the road. This is important because many times a ratio will only change slowly over time. Also, ratios can be influenced by demographics; for example, younger people generally have higher LTV and expense ratios while older people, especially those in their "peak earnings years," generally have lower LTV and expense ratios. Therefore, you should not be overly concerned if a ratio that you are using does not show immediate improvement. You also should not be overly confident if your ratios happen to be very strong. Rather,

Table 11.3 Modified Annual Household Budget Example

Line		
(a)	$55,000	Salary or wages
(b)	$21,000	Mortgage at $1,750 per month
(c)	$5,200	Food at $100 per week
(d)	$3,600	Utilities at $300 per month
(e)	$3,300	Phone and internet at $275 per month
(f)	$2,400	Car payment at $200 month
(g)	$4,000	Clothes, shoes and miscellaneous
(h)	$5,000	Donations
(i)	$10,000	Income taxes
(j)	$3,000	Real estate and car taxes
(k)	($2,500)	Debt needed to fund spending
(l)	**$32,200**	**Fixed Expenses: mortgage, food, utilities, car payment**
(m)	**$6,300**	**Discretionary: phone, internet, and $3,000 of miscellaneous**
(n)	**70.0%**	**Expense Ratio = ($32,200 + $6,300) / $55,000 salary**

Table 11.4 Modified Annual Household Budget Example—No Mortgage

Line		
(a)	$55,000	Salary or wages
(b)	$0	Mortgage—house paid off
(c)	$5,200	Food at $100 per week
(d)	$3,600	Utilities at $300 per month
(e)	$3,300	Phone and internet at $275 per month
(f)	$2,400	Car payment at $200 month
(g)	$4,000	Clothes, shoes and miscellaneous
(h)	$5,000	Donations
(i)	$10,000	Income taxes
(j)	$3,000	Real estate and car taxes
(k)	$18,500	Available for savings
(l)	**$11,200**	**Fixed Expenses: mortgage, food, utilities, car payment**
(m)	**$6,300**	**Discretionary: phone, internet, and $3,000 of miscellaneous**
(n)	**31.8%**	**Expense Ratio = ($11,200 + $6,300)/$55,000 salary**

consider the trend of the ratio, and how it relates or reconciles to your personal finance strategy. Over time, the two should clearly match. If yours do not match, you should find out why, and then take corrective measures to the extent that you can.

Our third and final dimension is in many ways the most important one: saving. In general, a savings rate of 5 to 10 percent of a person's annual income is indicative of financial wellness. However, this can be a very steep threshold for many households. Fortunately, there are ways to stimulate savings, such as through the income tax code.

Everyone is required to file an annual income tax return, which many (most) of us do not like to do. However, included in the income tax code are "credits," such as the "earned-income tax credit," which can be used by some people to legally increase their tax refund. Such refunds can, and should, be used to start or add-to savings accounts to the extent that is possible.

All of this may seem relevant to only lower income families, but it is not. Many mid-to-higher income families are also in need of greater levels of financial wellness awareness and many should seek tax advice. In fact, everyone needs to continuously work on both their physical and their financial wellness. Being "in shape" physically and financially is a worthy goal for everyone.

THE BACK-UP PLAN

We earlier mentioned that some jobs can generate a great deal of stress. However, for many people the loss of a job can be the cause of the most stress outside of a critical illness or the death of a loved one. In fact, in some cases, the loss of a job and the inability to find another one quickly, has led to destructive behavior such as alcohol, excessive gambling and substance abuse. In a few cases, such behavior has actually and unfortunately resulted in the untimely passing of people we know.

One way to mitigate the stress of losing a job is by having a back-up plan, which can be put into effect if a job loss occurs. Back-up plans can take many forms, but they all involve four basic elements. First is closing any potential skill-gap that you may have to both improve your performance in your current position, and to make you more marketable to future employers.

Second is creating, and then working with, a network of people who can help you identify career opportunities and potential job leads. Notice that we did not say using someone in your network to give you a job. That is generally not what networks are for. A personal network is a source of information, including potential leads, which may lead to an employment opportunity. The reason for this is that many people are more than willing to provide information that could be helpful, but they in general do not like being solicited for work. Always keep this in mind when networking. Additionally, you should keep in touch with people in your network regularly, not just when you may need something.

Third is thinking through the businesses that you could speak with about a position if you happen to lose your job. One helpful aid in doing this is to create a short-list of businesses, which should be reviewed regularly to ensure that it is up to date in the event you need it. As part of these activities, you should regularly monitor the work/career environment for potential opportunities.

The final element is preparing a list of resources that you can tap for help during a job search. Examples include career coaches, professional resume writers, job search websites, and trade associations.

Creating back-up plans may seem to be a lot of work. However, recall the late Andy Grove's words that we quoted in Chapter 5:

> The sad news is, nobody owes you a career. Your career is literally your business. You own it as a sole proprietor. You have one

employee: yourself. You are in competition with millions of similar businesses: millions of other employees all over the world. You need to accept ownership of your career, your skills, and the timing of your moves. It is your responsibility to protect this personal business of yours from harm and to position it to benefit from changes in the environment. Nobody else can do that for you.

Having a back-up plan is a key part of protecting your personal business from long-term harm, and for positioning it to benefit from the environmental changes that *will* occur over time. While these plans are important for everyone, they are especially important for people with disabled dependents, which is the subject we turn to next.

WELLNESS AND DISABILITIES

According to the *Centers for Disease Control and Prevention (CDC)*, approximately 1 in every 33 children is born with a birth defect. A list of the most frequent birth defects, as well as related information, can be found at the CDC's website: www.cdc.gov/ncbddd/birthdefects/data.html.

Birth defects are, of course, not the only cause of disabilities. Illness and accidents can also cause disabilities, as can law enforcement/fire and military injuries, as well as severe forms of substance abuse, and various other things. This is significant because it reflects the sad fact that disabilities impact a far larger number of Americans than one in every 33 families. Equally significant, there is nothing on the horizon to suggest that these probabilities will be reversing any time soon.

Financial wellness is urgently important when a disabled dependent is involved. Foremost amongst the many considerations of caring for disabled people is the choice and funding of medical care. In general, the best medical care can be found in teaching hospitals. In addition to superior doctors, teaching hospitals tend to have deep levels of expertise with numerous insurance plans. They can also be accommodative in setting up payment plans for deductibles and other non-covered medical expenses involved in the care of a disabled person.

However, teaching hospitals may not accept all forms of medical insurance, including some governmentally provided medical insurance. For example, Joe's daughter is disabled and, as incredible as it may seem, neither his local teaching hospital nor any of her other doctors accepted the medical insurance that she was provided with as part of her Social Security Disability benefits. When something like this happens, one should immediately push-back on the medical insurance they received. The initial stage of doing this involves working with your medical providers and governmental case worker(s) to obtain the medical care that the disabled dependent requires.

In general, doctors, hospital administrators, and many elected officials are often, albeit not always, eager to help with disability-related insurance and financial disputes, but you must have your facts straight before you speak with them. This means clearly documenting who the health insurance provider is, why there is a problem with coverage, and so on. Being fact-based is also critically important given the stress levels involved. Watching disabled people, especially children, struggle through day-to-day activities exerts extreme amounts of emotional stress, which can affect people in numerous ways.

Stress levels can rise dramatically when intensive medical treatments like surgery are required, especially when children are involved. It can be particularly tempting during times like this to use luxury spending as a kind of emotional therapy. For example, we know many families with disabled children that have incurred significant amounts of debt to fund elaborate vacations following stressful periods in their lives. It is understandable to want nice vacations to relieve emotional stress. However, taking on a great deal of debt to fund such vacations can, over time, increase one's financial stress. Left unchecked, elevated stress levels can—and have—caused families to break up, including and especially families with disabled dependents. This is not to say that vacations are not important; in fact, they can be very important, but they do not need be expensive or extravagant to reduce emotional stress.

One way to reduce overall stress levels is to avoid financial stress altogether, to the extent that is possible. This can be accomplished, for example, by closely following personal budgets and monitoring expense ratios, which were discussed earlier. Tracking monthly budgets and expense ratios can help to control non-essential spending when money is not readily available to fund it. It can also help to fund luxury-related spending by explicitly saving for such spending over time, rather than making purchases "on time" via the use of credit.

In sum, disabilities are emotionally stressful, and they can also be financially stressful, which is a fact that is not always appreciated or managed. Personal expense management will obviously not resolve all disability-related financial issues, but it can help to prevent such issues from getting worse.

NOTE

1 Alan Kline, "Household Debt Hit Another All-Time High: Is It Poised to Level Off?" *American Banker*, Undated, www.americanbanker.com/list/household-debt-hit-another-all-time-high-is-it-poised-to-level-off

12

PERSONAL INVESTING

One way to ease both the pressure of personal expenses, and the siren song of easy credit, is by having either supplementary income or investment income that can help to fund desired purchases. To generate investment income, you need an investment portfolio. The larger the portfolio, the greater the amount of investment income that is generally available.

Some people with large portfolios are born into wealth. Others build such portfolios through working in the entertainment industry, sports industry, or a high paying profession. Most people, however, build their investment portfolios over time by working long and hard at traditional jobs, and then investing part of their saved earnings. Over time, the value of such portfolios can appreciably grow as returns compound and money continues to be added to the portfolios. We discussed compounding in Chapter 2 so if you need a refresher on this all-important subject, please refer to that chapter before reading on.

While some people have been able to successfully invest their money themselves, that is growing continuously harder to do as the scope of financial products grows, and their complexity deepens. There are also legions of professional money managers, some better than others obviously, but all devote their entire working hours to investing in the financial markets. They are, therefore, formidable competition for all amateur investors. As a result, we suggest that you retain professional money managers to oversee your investment portfolios.

Here are some things to consider when you are selecting an investment or money manager:

DOI: 10.4324/9781003215417-13

- The manager: Who is managing your money, what is their track record, and who is auditing their work? In general, an independent firm should audit a money manager's books, and that auditor should be large and well-respected to ensure that they have ample amounts of "errors and omissions" insurance to pay any legal claims that may be filed against them for failing to properly audit the books. This is important. The most successful money managers that we know have stellar tracks records that are readily available to inspect, and they are audited by top global accounting firms. Also, most (if not all) of these investors' own money is invested in the funds that they manage. Positive factors like these do not mean that your funds are not at risk of loss, of course: *all investment funds are always at risk of loss*. It does, however, mean that your funds are in very good hands, and as such, your portfolio should perform well over time, which will put the power of compounding to work for you.
- Assets under management (AUM): Money managers with large AUM generally have good reputations, which they want to maintain. They also generally have large amounts of insurance to pay legal claims. These factors can mitigate the risk of fraud or an "error of omission," which could result in a loss. If you choose to deal with smaller money managers, and some smaller managers are very good, it is important to: (1) verify the existence and amounts of insurance that they carry, and (2) place only a portion of your funds under management with them.
- Investment approach: It is crucial to understand exactly how a money manager intends to invest your money. Once you know this, you can benchmark, monitor, and evaluate their performance over time. This is very important, but it is often overlooked. Your money managers work for you. Therefore, they should be monitored and if their performance is not to your standards, they should be replaced.

DO NOT PUT ALL YOUR EGGS IN ONE BASKET

Despite how careful your manager selection process may be, personal investing and financial mistakes can still be made. For example, in addition to outright fraud, investment losses can be caused by poor corporate management, tight credit conditions, and when many seemingly unrelated things go wrong at the same time—which occurs more often than you may think. Losses can also occur when the stock market in general goes down. For example, during the 2007–2008 global financial crisis, many investment losses were incurred. More severe losses were suffered by people who invested in firms within the housing and financial sectors, especially the firms in those sectors that failed due to poor corporate governance and suboptimal business practices. At the present time, it is unclear what the longer-term financial ramifications of the coronavirus pandemic will be on publicly held stocks and bonds.

One way to mitigate the risk of an outsized investment loss is not to concentrate your investment funds in any one investment, or with any one investment manager. Here are five things to consider when diversifying your investment funds.

First, it is important to understand that diversification is a way to generate a desired overall investment return over time. Therefore, you should not expect to "get rich quickly." In fact, it is a good practice to avoid anyone who says that they can help you "get rich quickly" because they simply cannot.

Second, there are many ways to diversify an investment portfolio. For example, you can diversify across "asset classes" such as equities (stocks), bonds, and real estate. You can also diversify within an asset class—for example, by buying an equity portfolio composed of biotechnology, entertainment, and industrial stocks. A basic level of diversification entails the following:

- A savings account with enough cash in it to fund your lifestyle for at least three months, and preferably for up to one year or more. This is an emergency fund, which is insured through the Federal Deposit Insurance Corporation (FDIC) up to $250,000, that you can use if you find yourself suddenly out of a job or if you find yourself saddled with a sudden, large expense that was not budgeted for. Cash can also be used to selectively take advantage of highly lucrative investment opportunities when they arise.
- A retirement account with some mix of credit (bills, notes, and bonds) and equity (stock) investments. Historically, the default investment portfolio has been 60 percent in credit and 40 percent in equities, but this allocation should only be used as a very rough guideline. Actual portfolio percentages vary widely by

individual and household so we cannot provide a specific suggestion here. A licensed financial advisor from a large, well-regarded financial planning firm can help you to think through different diversification strategies, especially those involving annuities and other life insurance products. Such products sometimes guarantee specific return levels and, significantly, the guarantees are from large, highly credit-rated insurance companies, which can make them relatively attractive to some people. However, regardless of the path that you choose, never forget that advisors only advise. All investment decisions are yours to make and monitor.

Third, diversification also applies to investment managers. Different managers can be hired—and again, do not ever forget that they all work for you—to invest in equities, credit, real estate, and other asset classes. As we have stated several times in this book, you should generally only invest with large money management firms.

Fourth, as your investment portfolio grows, consider spreading your funds across both asset classes and money managers who invest differently within asset classes. For example, one equity manager who invests in growth stocks and another who invests in value (or underpriced) stocks.

Fifth, diversification requires careful monitoring and discipline over time. For example, when a particular investment, asset class, and/or money manager is significantly over-performing you may have to allocate funds away from that investment, asset class, and/or manager to comply with your long-term diversification strategy. This will not be easy for many people, but like all good things, diversification is not easy. However, when it is done well it will help to mitigate the risk of loss over time.

BEWARE OF GUARANTEES

As you likely know by now, the risk of loss can be incredibly wide and involves acts that are accidental as well as those that are intentional. Accidents happen every day because human beings are only human, and therefore prone to error. Intentional acts of wrongdoing also happen frequently, and therefore they should be guarded against. This applies to both corporate and personal finance.

We recently spoke with someone who was defrauded in an investment. This person had a very successful career in corporate finance before he retired. So, when we questioned him about how he came to be defrauded, we were somewhat surprised when he stated: "The thing that really threw me was that the investment was guaranteed!" Our friend took this verbal guarantee at face value, which is something that you should never do. Just because someone may say that an investment is "guaranteed" does not mean that it is.

There are four basic kinds of financial guarantees: The first is a form of insurance policy known as a performance bond. The second is a trust that is established to specifically fund a guarantee, which is typically managed by a bank or licensed accounting or law firm. The third kind of guarantee is provided by the government. An example of a governmental financial guarantee is the Federal Deposit Insurance Corporation (FDIC), which guarantees bank savings accounts up to $250,000. The fourth guarantee is an unsecured guarantee, which means that nothing back-stops the guarantee except the promise of the person or firm that is making it.

Here is a practical way of evaluating nongovernmental financial guarantees. You first must establish the nature of a guarantee; meaning, is it based on some kind of insurance/performance bond or is it via a trust? If neither of these is in place, then the guarantee you are considering is unsecured. If an investment is a fraud, then any guarantee made by the fraudster is also fraudulent. This may sound like common sense, but it is often overlooked when people are presented with lucrative investment returns that are "guaranteed." This is the reason why, when we mentioned annuity return guarantees earlier, we noted that the firms making those guarantees were "large, highly credit-rated insurance companies." Such companies have every incentive to deliver on their guarantees, and if they fail to do so, they have ample assets, as well as large amounts of errors and omissions insurance, to target in a lawsuit.

If there is a bond or trust in place, the next step is to get information on it such as the name of the firm that issued the bond or that is managing the trust, the date it began, the date it ends, the face value of the bond or trust, the extent to which that value has been/may be eroded by claims, and any conditions for making prospective claims.

While all this may seem like a great deal of information, it is all very basic, and as a result it can all be easily faked. Therefore, all information that you are provided *must* be independently validated.

Common methods of validating financial guarantees include comprehensive legal and credit reviews. This can be costly, so one way to reduce the cost is to do some of the legwork yourself. For example, you can look up contact information for insurance companies, banks, accounting firms, and law firms, and either call or visit them to validate any information that you have been provided.

You can also contact local regulatory agencies, such as state Insurance Departments, and consumer advocacy groups, such as the Better Business Bureau, to determine if an insurance company, bank, accounting firm, or law firm is in good standing. Similarly, you can check the internet as well as social media websites to track cyber complaint activity and trends.

If you accomplish all these activities and determine that a particular financial guarantee seems valid, you should then have a lawyer review it for you. There is a cost to do this properly, but it is important to legally validate the status of any financial guarantee before making an investment, especially a sizeable investment. Mitigating the risk of loss, including loss caused by investment fraud, is a big part of long-term financial-and physical-wellness.

OTHER KINDS OF INVESTMENTS

Investments can take many forms. We were recently speaking with someone about this and were surprised when they mentioned that they viewed lotteries as a form of investment. When we asked them why they felt this way, they replied, "For only a dollar you actually have a chance to win millions! You don't get chances like that in the stock market."

Nearly every state in the United States has a lottery. This is not surprising since the lottery is, in many ways, a politician's dream— a tax that is both voluntary and creates significant revenue. With such political advantages, coupled with the reality that only a few individuals will win huge sums of money, there is little wonder that lotteries have become so prevalent. Despite their prevalence, however, lotteries have a cost, and those who are most affected by these costs are from lower-income communities.

Numerous studies have confirmed that lower-income workers, and generally less educated people, spend far more money on lottery tickets than the wealthy or well educated. Economically, this effectively creates, for those who are poor and participate heavily in lotteries, a reverse tax bracket where the poor are taxed at the highest rates.

In 2011, after the last recession, many states set lottery sales records, which led some state "officials [to] acknowledge the lottery appears to be recession-proof."[1] This indicates that during hard times, when personal and family budgets are at their tightest, people spend money on something that is virtually guaranteed to give them nothing in return. Had these people instead invested the money that they spent on lottery tickets during this period, they would

DOI: 10.4324/9781003215417-14

likely have had a substantial positive return on their investments as the financial markets went on to recover from the recession lows. Instead, almost everyone who bought lottery tickets during 2010, and afterwards, lost every penny they spent.

Here is why: the probability of winning a simple lottery, which pays off for six correct numbers out of 49, is 1-in-13,983,816.[2] For Powerball lotteries the odds are even worse and have been calculated at 1-in-146,107,962 (we will not display these calculations as they are a little more involved). What do these extreme probabilities tell us? It is more likely we will die by being struck by lightning than it is we will win the lottery.

Lotteries are therefore a game of chance, not an investment. All games of chance have winners. So, what about them? Various studies have confirmed that lottery winners have suffered many problems, including bankruptcy.[3] The most likely reason for this is the fact that many lottery players are poorer, less educated, and generally less financially literate. Therefore, in essence, lotteries provide large sums of money to very few individuals, many of whom do not have the skills to manage it properly over time.

Buying lottery tickets can also be addictive, like other forms of gambling or games of chance. This addiction can, of course, afflict both the rich and the poor, but lower-income people generally fare worse since lottery spending is a larger percentage of their earnings.

The possibility of instant wealth can drive individuals to buy many lottery tickets, even though they have virtually no chance of winning. For example, before one large Powerball lottery someone that we know bought $50 in tickets to "increase my chances of winning." We explained that the money she spent, which she could not readily afford, did not increase her chances of winning. She, of course, did not win the lottery.

An article published in December of 2019 claims that Americans spend over $1,000 every year on lottery tickets.[4] If people had invested those dollars, or otherwise saved them, the majority would be financially much better off than they are now, especially over time given the power of compounding.

In sum, you should avoid lotteries, and you should tell your family and friends to avoid them too. There is little justification for lotteries in modern society where the toll on lower-income people is far greater than the revenue benefit that is raised through ticket sales.

INVESTING IN COLLEGE

Attending college has become increasingly politicized. As a result, discussing the relative costs and benefits of a college education for a person has become somewhat contentious. This is unfortunate because, for many people, paying for college will be their second largest purchase, second only to their home.

Many people fund their college educations with debt, like the way they fund the purchase of a home. The trend of student debt has increased dramatically over the years. For example, student loan debt in the year 2020 hit a record $1.6 trillion.[5]

Ever increasing levels of student loan debt is not necessarily "bad," and could be good if the benefits realized exceed all of the costs. However, this is not always the case. For example, on recent business trips, we have both sat next to young people who were clearly on their way to basic training. When asked where they were going, one answered in that sort of nervous tone that anyone who has gone through basic training immediately recognizes, "Well . . . I joined the Navy and am heading to basic training."

"That's great. What led you to choose the Navy?"

"I really like submarines. Plus, I had to get a job. I have a lot of student loan debt and I couldn't get a job."

This response reasonably led us to ask, "Oh, you're going to be an officer?"

"I'm not going to be an officer. I didn't pass the test. I'm going in as a sailor and hopefully after a couple of years, I'll be able to take the test again on an in-service basis and become an officer."

This young man studied Sociology at an average university, and therefore he should have been educated to a level necessary to pass a military officer's examination. That did not occur, but instead of being angry he simply stated, "I really should have thought long and hard about what I wanted out of college before I went. I'll be paying for that mistake for a good long time to come."

One way to evaluate if college is "worth it" for you, or your young adult, is to prepare a list of expected costs and benefits. All college costs should be listed including tuition, dormitory costs, and the amount of money that could have been made, but will be forgone, if the choice is to go to college rather than to go to work.

On the benefit side, you should record the amount of money that you expect to make from the date that you land a job out of school. Many universities provide job placement statistics, if asked, especially for programs like engineering, accounting, and criminal justice.

But what about general programs of study like Sociology, the Arts or Humanities? The benefits of such programs can vary widely. For example, many people who studied these subjects have done fine in their careers. Others, however, have not done so well.

The process of carefully thinking through what you specifically want out of a college education before you enroll can help to focus attention on whether college is the best use of both your time and your money. If it is not, alternatives such as trade schools, and other forms of technical training, could be explored.

Significantly, there is absolutely no reason why college cannot be revisited later, after a few years of work. In fact, practical experience could help to bring educational interests into focus, and it could also help to uncover economical ways of funding those interests over time.

CHARITIES

A good friend recently asked us several questions about donating to a charity. As we were considering a response, she asked, "Isn't this a lot like selecting an investment?"

There are obvious differences between making an investment and donating to a charity. Primary amongst these is that charities are generally chosen to align with a person's belief system (religious/philosophical, social/cultural, medical/scientific, and educational) while investments are generally, albeit not always (and seemingly less so every year), belief agnostic. Aside from this, however, there are some similarities between donating to a charity and making an investment.

For example, all of the professional investors we know work incredibly hard to validate their assumptions prior to making an investment. This practice can also apply when considering a charity. For example, it could involve validating a charity's non-profit status prior to donating or volunteering time. Websites such as GuideStar (www.guidestar.org/) can be useful in such efforts, but internet searches are only a first step. For either large donations, or significant time commitments on your part, on-site due diligence should be conducted prior to offering support. This could initially include inspecting a charity's official documentation, and then confirming that it is both up-to-date and in good-standing with the authorities.

Attention could then turn to evaluating the managers of the charity, which is just as important as evaluating investment managers. Two key managerial behaviors to assess are candor and transparency.

Candor is "the quality of being honest and straightforward in attitude and speech and the ability to make judgments free from discrimination or dishonesty." Candid nonprofit managers clearly explain what their charity's mission and objective are, and then they honestly report how their actions have advanced their mission over time.

Financial transparency pertains to visibility in the way that managers spend their supporters' money. A transparent charity is one that both thoroughly discloses how it intends to spend its supporters' donations, and then reports in detail how it spent those donations over a given timeframe.

Superior charities, like superior investment funds, are led by managers who are both candid and transparent. One without the other is not necessarily "bad," but it may mean the presence of risk.

To understand why, consider the charity that a friend of ours was considering. It is managed by people who very candidly explained their mission, but they then stated that their policy was not to disclose how their supporters' donations have been spent. Our friend was rightly concerned about this and asked us if it sounded "right." It did not, and therefore we recommended that some due diligence was in order.

As part of the diligence process, we spoke with an experienced charity supporter. When our friend's situation was explained to this person, he stated that, "Without transparency it is impossible to assess the return on your charitable donation."

The term "return" is not often used in a nonprofit context, and as a result it somewhat surprised us. The expert that we were speaking with sensed this and continued his explanation.

> By return I mean the impact that your donation or time has on advancing the charity's mission, whatever that may be. If you

are not able to assess that, how do you know if your money and/or time have been well spent? Also, if you do not have some sense of return, how will you be able to compare and contrast the various charities that you may want to support?

After our discussion, we reported back to our friend and concluded our recommendations with the words of a well-known historical politician, "Trust but verify." You need to validate all of your assumptions in all kinds of investments, for-profit and not-for-profit alike.

Following this experience, we wrote a newspaper column on charitable donations. Interestingly, many people advised us not to write about fraud and charities, especially religious-based charities, because they considered it controversial. As we were deciding whether or not to do so, a good friend advised one of us that the potential controversy is exactly the reason why we should write such a piece. This we agreed with, so we wrote the column.

We then watched an episode of the popular television show, *American Greed*, which profiled a financial fraud perpetrated by a religious organization. That organization was funded by the charitable donations of its parishioners, as virtually all religious organizations are. However, this organization went on to set up an investment program for its parishioners. The marketing slogan that they used was, "Do good by doing good." However, the investment program turned out to be fraudulent, and many of the people who invested in it lost their money.

Religious frauds can be particularly devastating because many people do not exercise the level of skepticism in evaluating such investments as they otherwise would. Needless to say, we are not saying that you should not donate to religious-based charities or that you should not invest in religious-based investment programs. We are saying that you should be careful when considering a donation to any charity, and that you should be especially careful when making any kind of investment, as we discussed in the last chapter. Doing so will help to ensure that your intended charitable impact will be realized, and that your expected investment return will be earned over time.

NOTES

1 Joel Siegel, "State Lotteries Are Booming in Tough Times: Seventeen States Set Lottery Sales Records in the Past Year," *ABC News*, September 2 (2011), https://abcnews.go.com/Business/lottery-ticket-sales-surging-tough-economic-times/story?id=14435376

2 We provide the calculation to illustrate how precise this probability is estimated: 1-in-(49/6 * 48/5 * 47/4 * 46/3 * 45/2 * 44/1) equals 1-in-13,983,816. While this may appear complicated to some, it is only a string of basic multiplication and division.

3 Trilby Beresford, "Why It Sucks to Win the Lottery," *Grunge*, August 24 (2017), Updated February 2 (2021), www.grunge.com/82341/why-sucks-win-lottery/?utm_campaign=clip

4 Megan Leonhardt, "Americans Spend Over $1,000 a Year on Lotto Tickets," *CNBC Make It*, December 12 (2019), www.cnbc.com/2019/12/12/americans-spend-over-1000-dollars-a-year-on-lotto-tickets.html

5 Zack Friedman, "Student Loan Debt Statistics in 2020: A Record $1.6 Trillion," *Forbes*, February 3 (2020), www.forbes.com/sites/zackfriedman/2020/02/03/student-loan-debt-statistics/#78bedae5281f

CONCLUSION AND FIVE MORE COMMANDMENTS OF FINANCIAL WELLNESS

In Chapter 1 we offered our "Ten Commandments" of financial wellness. For ease of reading, we will list them again here:

1   The house you live in is your home, it is NOT a source of equity to "unlock" or an ATM-like repository of cash to spend. Your home is where you and your family live. Therefore, you should not use it as collateral for any loan outside of a first mortgage, absent some dire circumstance. To repeat, absent something dire, you should *never* put your home financially at risk.

2   Whenever you make a purchase, even a large purchase like a home or car, try to pay discount prices whenever possible. It will likely take time to find favorably priced assets and goods, but it is well worth both your time and your effort to do so. Sometimes a great "deal" will fall into your lap, but that is the exception rather than the rule. Normally, you have to work at it to find a discount.

3   Pay close attention to interest rates. This applies to both the interest rates that you pay (such as mortgage rates, car loan rates, and credit card rates) and the interest rates that you earn (from bank savings accounts, 401k plans, and individual retirement accounts). You should strive to earn more in interest income than you pay out in interest expense over time. The only way to accomplish this is to continuously work at it.

4   Limit the purchase of luxury goods and fund such purchases with cash rather than credit to the extent that you can. In general, you should only use consumer credit sparingly, and remember to watch the credit terms as well as the interest rates that you are charged when you do use it (as noted in commandment 3).

5 <u>Saving money is important</u>. The act of saving gets the power of "compounding" (or interest paid on interest, and investment returns that are earned on prior investment returns) working for you over time. Therefore, the sooner that you start to save, the better—even if the amounts that you save are small.

6 <u>Don't ever forget that there is NO easy way to become wealthy</u>. This is particularly important to remember when you are dealing with someone who tells you that they have a simple or easy way for you to become wealthy. People who say things like this either do not know what they are talking about and/or they are fraudsters. Whatever else you do after reading this book, please do *not* ignore this commandment!

7 <u>Size matters</u>. So, absent some very compelling reason, you should generally only invest with large money management firms. Large firms tend to have large assets of their own, and they have large amounts of insurance coverage to protect those assets if they are sued. Having assets and insurance available to pay legal judgments will help to mitigate the risk of fraud or loss if something goes wrong. Regrettably, things can, and often do, go wrong with investments for any number of reasons.

8 <u>Do not put all your investment eggs into one basket</u>. To the extent that your savings portfolio begins to grow, you should generally diversify your investment funds across different money management firms and asset classes. For example, have one money management firm invest stocks for you and another money management firm invest bonds for you. You should generally never have just one firm managing all your money.

9 <u>Ignore "the Joneses."</u> Many people feel under pressure to keep up with the spending patterns of family, friends, and celebrities. This is a mistake for a variety of reasons, primary amongst these is that the people you may be trying to keep up with may not have made well-thought-out purchases and/or may not have funded their purchases well. Therefore, you should fund the lifestyle that YOU want, not the one that you think someone else has.

10 <u>If you come to be defrauded, contact law enforcement officials immediately</u>. Do not delay because of feelings of embarrassment. You should never feel embarrassed, but rather take action quickly in the hope that you will get at least some of your money back, and that you will help to bring the fraudster to justice as quickly as possible.

Each of these "commandments" have been addressed across this book's various chapters, sometimes more than once. However, several other things have also been discussed that could be interpreted as "commandments." Therefore, to conclude this book, we will offer five additional commandments of financial wellness:

11 <u>Remember that finance is a means to an end</u>. The financial "end" in question is the lifestyle that you choose to live. Always remember to think carefully about how you will use the money that you earn, as opposed to merely trying to earn more of it. In general, more modest, and conservative lifestyles are both easier to fund, and generally less stressful over time, than grandiose lifestyles. We say "generally" because circumstances such as medical and legal expenses, for either yourself or for a close family member, can—and oftentimes do—generate a great deal of stress. Nevertheless, the central message of this "commandment" holds: Easily funded lifestyles will enable you to spend more of your time enjoying life than struggling to pay for it.

12 <u>Think for yourself</u>. One of us worked for the IBM Corporation many years ago. During the onboarding process, we were presented with several items that had the word, THINK, written on them. When we inquired why, we learned that THINK is the company's longstanding motto. When we asked why this was their motto, we were told, "Because so few people really think, we have an advantage when all of our employees think." Somewhat incredibly, this statement has a wide level of applicability across both corporate and personal finance. For example:

- You should give serious thought to the life that you want to live, not the life that you think other people want you to live.
- If you think that a trade education is a better choice for you at the present time than a college education, then that is what you should do regardless of what others may think or say.
- If your family and friends are pouring their money into an investment that, for whatever reason, does not seem right to you, then you should not invest in it regardless of what "they" may think, and so on.

In sum, when it comes to finance, don't ever let anyone tell you how to think, and that includes family, friends, advisors, professors, politicians of both parties, entertainers, as well as influencers on social media. THINK for yourself!

13 <u>Protect yourself at all times</u>. In many sports—amateur and professional alike—the athletes are instructed to protect themselves at all times. This is also incredibly good advice when it comes to finance. Doubt, as well as a healthy dose of radical skepticism, are traits that the very best professional investors use to safeguard the money that is under their care from the risk of loss. Expressing these traits does not always lead to profit, of course, as loss is a fact of life. However, these traits can limit the number of times that you are wrong, and the amount of money that you lose when you are wrong.

14 <u>No one can predict the future, but everyone can prepare for it</u>. One of us recently spoke with someone who claimed to have a mathematical model that was "incredibly predictive of the future." With a smile, we responded that this type of claim has been made many times in the past and has always proven erroneous. To be clear, no one can predict the future, which is the basis for the rightly famous statement that, "all models are wrong, some models are useful." However, everyone can prepare for the future and, significantly, you do not need a model to do it! Key preparation activities include thinking hard about the choices and trade-offs that life throws at you (commandment 12), protecting yourself at all times (commandment 13), and not wasting time trying to predict what the future may hold (commandment 14).

15 <u>Your finances, including your job/career, are your responsibility</u>. Early in one of our careers, one of us worked for a particularly incompetent manager. One day this person instructed us to, "just work hard, and leave your career to me!" No one should ever leave their career to another person, so we did not. In addition, we are convinced that no one should say anything like this to someone else. Regardless of whether you work for an incompetent manager like we unfortunately did, or a superb one, always remember that the course of your career is your responsibility, and yours alone. The same, of course, applies to your spending and saving activities.

CONCLUSION

We will close this book with the profile of a person who has lived each of our 15 commandments. His story will help to illustrate the impact of the concepts that we have profiled. We will refer to this person as "Dwight." He is a Vietnam War combat veteran. When he returned home from the war, Dwight got married, and worked in construction. While he liked construction, the job offered no medical or retirement benefits. As Dwight enjoyed being in uniform, he joined the Army Reserve with an eye on the future benefits it provides.

Three children followed, and Dwight left construction to join the maintenance department of a local industrial plant. He and his family lived frugally, but they also lived well. Over time, Dwight was promoted to maintenance supervisor at the plant, and he also rose in the ranks of the Army Reserve, so much that his monthly drill salary came to cover his monthly mortgage payments. To reduce his mortgage, Dwight paid an extra 10 percent on it each month. Making this payment greatly reduced the duration of his mortgage, which was relatively quickly paid off. Of course, he continued to actively save for his retirement across his career.

Following the tragic September 11 terrorist attacks, Dwight was recalled to active duty. As he was headed overseas, we ran into him in an airport that we were both traveling through. Sometimes happy coincidences do happen! At any rate, given his age, Dwight was not involved in combat, but he did serve in a warzone. In doing so, he was one of, if not the, last Vietnam War combat veterans in active service.

When he returned home from overseas, Dwight retired as a maintenance supervisor in the plant that he worked in, and as a Sergeant Major in the Army Reserve, which is the highest rank available to non-commissioned officers. We saw Dwight recently, and he continues to enjoy retirement with his wife and family.

When we asked him how he accomplished all that he did, his reply was: "Focus on the lifestyle that you want, both while you are working and when you are retired, and then work to fund it being careful to stay out of debt as you age."

Dwight is an amazing person for a number of reasons, but financially we can all learn a great deal from him.

With our very best wishes for a happy and financially solvent life!

INDEX

Note: Page locators in **bold** indicate a table.

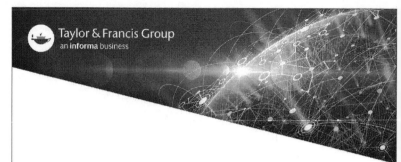